ADOLF HITLER

Adolf Hitler 1923.

ADOLF HITLER

Compiled by Maurice E. Kelly

Translated by Inge Christl

Universal Books Ltd.

TRANSLATOR'S NOTE

"Adolf Hitler — Pictures from the Life of the Fuhrer" as published in Germany, 1936, with the endorsement of the NSDAP, was a massive work of propaganda designed to glorify the Fuhrer, his work and achievements, and his plans for Germany. It contains contributions by leading National Socialist figures, including Joseph Goebbels, Rudolph Hess, Albert Speer and Robert Ley.

These major propagandists extolled the virtues and activities of Hitler, thus elevating him to a superhuman, or god—like status.
Each section deals with an aspect of Hitler's life or work, from his travels and his private life, his prowess as an orator or as a statesman, his interest in architecture and the arts, to his involvement with the army and the Hitler Youth.

This translation has attempted to capture the atmosphere of the language of the National Socialist era, and as such, must be viewed as an important historical document and a chilling example of the power of fanaticism and propaganda.

We are unable, my Fuhrer, to express our thanks in words. We are also unable to reveal our loyalty and our affection to you through words. All our gratitude, our love and our fervent trust in you, my Fuhrer, can be seen glowing in the hundreds of thousands of faces turned towards you today.

All our people, our whole nation, today feel strong and happy because in you there has arisen not only the Fuhrer of the nation, but also the Saviour of the Nation.

The Reichstag's President before the German Reichstag at Nuremberg on the 15th September, 1935.

Goring

Published by
Universal Books Ltd.
The Grange Grange Yard
London SEI 3AG

National Library of Australia
Cataloguing-in-publication

Adolf Hitler.

ISBN 0 908240 88 0.

1. Hitler, Adolf, 1889-1945. 2. National socialism -
Biography. 3. Germany - Politics and government -
1933-1945 - Biography. I. Kelly, Maurice (Maurice
Edward). II. Christl, Inge.

943.086'092'4

Printed by
Gráficas Reunidas, S. A.
Avda. de Aragón, 56
28027 Madrid

𝕿able 𝕺f Contents

2nd August, 1914 at Odeonsplatz, Munich (Adolf Hitler
in the middle of the enthusiastic throng).

PREFACE

The idea of propaganda is associated the world over and even still in Germany today with a host of misconceptions. These misconceptions are so deeply rooted, and often linked with prejudices, that they can only be clarified with difficulty. Of all people, it is the Germans who, since the War, have learnt a lesson from experience in this respect. In this relatively short period of time propaganda in Germany has proved itself to be a politically powerful force of the first order. Today no further proof is needed that the Germany under the Kaisers was being under—mined by Marxist propaganda, and that the Marxist-democratic regime was able to be removed because it was opposed by a superior new order and power, expounded not only by the National Socialist doctrine but also by National Socialist propaganda.

Propaganda must also be masterful. It is pointless to direct a few resourceful men into this area now and then. As with every great art form, there are men who are particularly skilled at propaganda, who usually establish a school and then become its teachers. That there is some—thing dishonourable or despicable about propaganda is a widespread misconception which should be put aside. As in every field of human endeavour, the important thing is what is being sup—ported and what propaganda brings to the practical world. In this sense it has nothing to do with publicity. At its best it lets issues and people speak for themselves and ensures that, if they are of value, then they will also be portrayed and elucidated in their full value.

Good things and great people have their own effect. They must therefore be allowed to speak freely for themselves. The most important characteristic of particularly successful propa—ganda is that it neither omits nor adds anything which does not belong to the essential nature of the subject. The characteristic feature of events and personalities should be brought out clearly, distinctively and simply, stripped bare of confusing details, so that they may be readily under—stood and recognized by the masses whom the propaganda is attempting to reach.

National Socialism and its principal representatives have brought along to this art form a natural talent. They have also learnt their trade and applied it through hard work, untiring, close contact with the people and a continual refining of the techniques involved. The Fuhrer himself was the greatest master in this process. It is not widely known that in the early days of the Party he held no other office than that of head of propaganda, and that in his brilliant mastery of this office he gave the Party its present intellectual, organisatory and political stamp.

He has always instinctively understood how to speak and deal with his people, whose child he has always been and will always be. From an early time, all the love and immense trust of his followers, and later of the whole of the German nation, has been focused on him. Yet initially the masses saw him from a distance only as a politician and statesman. His purely humane side remained largely in the background.

Today the whole world recognizes him as the initiator of the National Socialist doctrine and the creator of the National Socialist state, the pioneer of a new European order and the guide to peace and the welfare of nations. But behind this recognition countless millions of people the world over suspect that there is a fascinating and compelling personality behind the facade of the man Adolf Hitler. Germans and non-Germans alike have been captured by the great simplic—ity and simple greatness which this man radiates. He can probably be designated as the man who in all the world is most deeply and clearly rooted in the feelings and thoughts of our modern time, and is therefore capable as no other man to give this time a new shape and direction.

In order to understand him completely, one must know him not only as a politician and a statesman, but also as a human being. It is to this end that the book has been written. It is a testimony to his personality and has been compiled with affection and admiration by his closest colleagues and his oldest fellow combatants. They have put pen to paper to show the public an intimate picture of this great man. They have all known the Fuhrer closely for many years and have learnt to admire him anew on a daily basis. This is what constitutes the actual worth of this book.

In this book the Fuhrer is presented in his immediate relationship to all the issues of our time. The German people will seize this opportunity of seeing the Fuhrer at close range and personally getting to know him more closely.

It is pleasing to note that the book may be acquired simply and without great cost, a fact which will make it accessible to the masses of the German readership. May it find a happy and successful path into the German Nation!

Dr. Joseph Goebbels

The Fuhrer promotes aviation by his example.

The Fuhrer's Travels

by SS-Brigadier Fuhrer Julius Schreck

Never before has a leading statesman got to know his country and his people as thoroughly as has Adolf Hitler. Whether by motor vehicle, aeroplane or train, his travels always served his purpose, which was to acquaint himself thoroughly with his people.

Already at the beginning of his movement he was far-sighted in recognising the importance of rapid means of transport, particularly the motor vehicle which he used at that time despite its still rudimentary state of development. Even today the Fuhrer still prefers the motor vehicle because he considers it important to remain in constant contact with his national comrades and his old soldiers.

At the time of the great political struggles for power it was evident that the Fuhrer was far ahead of all his opponents due to the motorisation of his forces. There were not always crowds of enthusiastic people around the Fuhrer cheering him on then. In those years we experienced many a journey where the going was very tough and we could only secure our way through our presence of mind and through force.

No alarm signals could stop the Fuhrer from driving into the strongholds of his red and black opponents, often right through desolate scattered villages of Bolshevist organisations, past protesting marchers. Sometimes our car was totally surrounded by thousands of fellow countrymen who had been incited to violence. However, it was our experience that, again and again, at the sight of the Fuhrer these people would suddenly drop their raised fists. They would look up and realize that this Hitler looked completely different from the one who had always been described to them. How many misled workers at that time looked for the first time into the eyes of the man who was supposed to be their opponent, only to become immediate and fanatical followers of his movement? No amount of propaganda in the newspapers, and no books alone, could have brought about this miracle. And so, three years after his seizure of power, he could say: "Where is the statesman who, after three years of rule, need not fear to go out among his people as I do?"

When his work and his official duties permit it, then you will find the Fuhrer not only sitting in his office, but driving out into the country amidst his people. Sitting in his Mercedes again, he will appear sometimes here, sometimes there; one day in the Ruhr, the next in Baden, Wurttemberg, Saxony, East Prussia, at the coast. In brief, there is no district where his travels do not take him at least once. At the wheel of the car behind the windscreen, I then suddenly hear the amazed and enthusiastic cries: "It's Hitler" or "The Fuhrer is here". Often the people do not even notice who has just driven through the town. Not until the convoy has moved on do

Trip through a small Franconian town.

The Fuhrer in Franconia, at the
war memorial in Hiltpoltstein
(Franconian Switzerland)

During a trip through Germany in his first car, his seat was already next to the driver.

On his journeys through Germany the Fuhrer prefers an open vehicle.

they become aware of the three black cars, and then all at once they realize who has just driven past. The children are in the main the first to recognize the Fuhrer. The moment this happens there is a race with the car, and then in a little while people gather around the car, several streets are alerted and finally we will have to stop a number of times so that the Fuhrer can shake hands with enthusiasts, accept flowers offered to him and at times autograph a few cards.

Whoever has been fortunate enough, as I have been, to be constantly by the Fuhrer's side and participate in his many journeys, will have thousands of unforgettable pictures imprinted in his mind in the course of the years. Such journeys leave you with an enormous belief in the German people and an immense feeling of warmth.

Major journeys are undertaken by the Fuhrer only in an open vehicle, which he refuses to close even if it rains in the course of an official visit. To the advice of his entourage his only response is always: "As long as the SA and the other groups have to stand in the rain, we can get wet as well." Thousands were witnesses as he inspected, bare headed and dressed only in his brown shirt, the march-past of the SA at the reintegration of the Saar, as he spoke to the waiting crowds in pouring rain after a night flight at three o'clock in the morning at the election campaigns in Stralsund, or drove in the rain through Holstein to the Adolf-Hitler-Koog, with no consideration for himself, because the SA was also standing in the rain.

Farewell from the NSDAP to Julius Schreck

The National Socialist Movement today takes leave of Julius Schreck. It takes leaves of one of its oldest and most faithful members. It takes leave of one of its best and most irreplaceable members. It takes leave of one of its most modest members, who wanted nothing for himself, who gave everything for Germany and for the Fuhrer.

When it was a question of fighting for Germany he stood at the front, whether it was in the World War or at home.

Boundless was his admiration and his love for the Fuhrer, untiring his concern for the Fuhrer, prudent his care for the protection of the Fuhrer.

His nature radiated dependability to the last. His presence spread a feeling of security among his party members in times of difficult struggle.

Unerring was his judgement of people, unequivocal his affection as was his aversion. A tough old warhorse with a warm heart. Feared by his opponents, loved by all who considered him one of themselves, honoured as a fatherly friend by his subordinates.

He had the good fortune of enjoying the highest trust of his Fuhrer. The Movement lowers its flags in a last greeting to Julius Schreck. In doing so, it swears to him that his behaviour and his spirit will be an example to the young and to generations to come, and that he will thus serve the Movement in the many years that lie ahead to the glory of our great National Socialist Germany.

RUDOLF HESS

Julius Schreck (died 16/5/1936)

11

Trip through the Harz. Even the Fuhrer can be cheerful.

Rest in the forest.

12

The Fuhrer on a flight.

On top of the Wartburg.

Today, after fifteen years, as chancellor of the Reich he has not given up this habit. He also determines the route himself, because the Fuhrer loves to use the side streets and experience Germany's countryside away from the major highways.

Before, when the Fuhrer was not as well known as today, it was often easier. Then there were times when we could spend the night or have a meal in a small inn. Today it is quite different. The news of the arrival of the Fuhrer spreads like wildfire in the villages and towns through which we pass. Many people are overjoyed and telephone the next village to pass on the news, and then the villagers, who have not yet seen their Fuhrer, will be waiting at the entrance of the town to greet Hitler as he arrives. There are then such impressive moments that many a time I have wished I were a poet so that I could find the words to describe the myriad of minor occurrences with the impact with which I experienced them.

We arrive in a town. Everyone is there, the old and the young, mothers with young children in their arms, clubs and schools. The main street is quickly transformed into a sea of flags. The girls in the BDM try to stop the car, but time is pressing and the Fuhrer must be at his destination

Travelling.

In the German countryside. Hiltpoltstein (Franconian Switzerland).

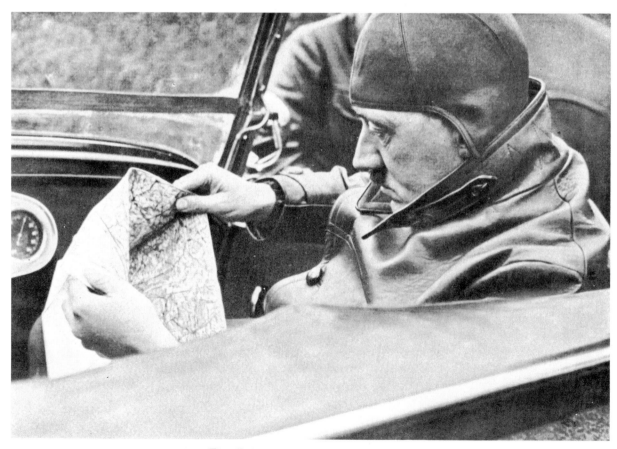

The Fuhrer determines the route.

14

at a certain time because hundreds of thousands in the gathering will be waiting for him. Then a large strapping fellow, the blacksmith of the village, suddenly jumps onto the bonnet of the car; now the Fuhrer is forced to slow down his trip and already the car is surrounded by the villagers. Everyone wants to shake the Fuhrer's hand. Women with children in their arms cannot get close. They hold their children, Germany's future, above the heads of the enthusiastic crowds, as if they wanted to say: You belong to him!

If one wants to describe great men, one also has to see their smaller traits. One of a hundred such episodes comes to mind. It is around ten o'clock at night as the Fuhrer is driving towards Wurzburg after a march-past in Meiningen. Then, in the glow of the headlights, we see two SA men marching along. The Fuhrer stops the car. They are asked where they are going. "To the nearest railway station. My comrade can't walk much further. We still have three hours ahead of us." "Then jump in!" They have no idea whose guests they are. We ask them a number of trivial questions. Then we ask them if they have already seen the Fuhrer. "Yes, today, during the march-past". The car stops, we have reached our destination. The Fuhrer, who is sitting in the front, calls to them and presses a sum of money into their hands. Then, in the darkness of the night, a small ray of light illuminates the Fuhrer face. The two SA men are paralysed. Wasn't it the Fuhrer, who had just spoken to them? Yes, it's him! No words can pass their lips. They are overcome by joy. I put my foot on the accelerator and we drive off into the dark night. As we turn a curve we see the two of them still standing motionless on the side of the road, dumbfounded by what they have just experienced.

The D—2600 above Nuremberg.
Arrival at the party conference of the Reich.

Election trip through Germany.

The major election campaigns at that time required the Fuhrer to utilize his time to the maximum, and so the Fuhrer would often make use of aircraft. This was at a time when air-traffic was still a cause for apprehension. For weeks on end aircraft would take him from town to town, with no consideration for wind or bad weather.

Looking back at this time I experience a slight shudder when I remember the numerous flights through storms, fog and dark nights. It says a lot that at the time when the aircraft figured prominently in the Fuhrer's election campaign the schedule for the take-off was never changed. Every meeting which had been planned - and at times there were 4-5 in various towns in Germany on the one day - was carried through on time.

Often the Fuhrer was advised not to go through with a certain flight. However, his answer was always: "If need be, then I will also fly through a storm". How the opposition would have rejoiced at that time if the scheduled flight plan had not been carried out or a planned meeting had been cancelled. But Hitler did not do them that favour.

Of these flights one in particular has stayed in my memory. This was the flight from Furth to Frankfurt. The old Rohrbach, the first machine which the Fuhrer used at that time, was anchored with fuel drums. Over the whole of Germany there was a storm the intensity of which we rarely experienced. All general air traffic was banned. Only with difficulty could we walk upright. Everyone shook their head when the Fuhrer boarded the aircraft. Yet, after a few minutes, it was already struggling to take off. Laboriously the aircraft made its way through thunderstorms, heavy gusts of rain and snow. Often the aircraft would suddenly plunge and the heads of many of the passengers hit the roof, but each time the flight continued successfully. Once the plane was forced to make an unscheduled emergency landing long before we reached our destination. The meeting in Kiel was to begin at 8 o'clock. At 5 o'clock I was informed that the Fuhrer had had to land at Travemunde due to the low clouds, fog and severe storms. Immediately the convoy sped off towards Lubeck and near Eutin we were to pick up the Fuhrer who was driving towards us in a hire car and bring him to Kiel on time.

Even if nowadays due to the pressures of time, the Fuhrer avails himself of train travel now and again on his night journeys, his great love is still for the motor vehicle, of which he himself once said that it opened up Germany for him. Likewise his love is for his Ju 52 under the command of captain SS Oberfuhrer Baur, who must number among the first geniuses of flight captains. The most pleasurable thing for the Fuhrer is when, after many strenuous weeks, he can once again drive through the German country in his car. The most pleasurable days for me are then when I can sit behind the wheel and, as once through war and deprivation, now drive the Fuhrer through a happy and peaceful country.

On the Buckeberg for the harvest festival of 1934.

The Fuhrer leaves the Landsburg Fortress, 1924.

Women from Buckeburg in their festival costumes during the
harvest festival in 1934.

The Fuhrer and the German People
by Dr Otto Dietrich

The relationship of the German people to the Fuhrer is a constant source of joyous pride to the Germans themselves and a cause of amazement and surprise for the rest of the world. Nowhere else in the world will you find such a fanatical love of millions of people for one man, a love which is not excessive, nor ecstatic, but rather the result of an immense and deep trust, a supreme confidence, such as children sometimes have for a very good father.

Enthusiasm lasts for only a few years; this love from the depths of the soul, however, once manifested, is indestructible and will last for centuries. It is like a large, powerful flame, re-markable for its constancy. It is a love which has not suddenly flared up or been lit by un-expected and stirring events, but one which has grown slowly and insistently. It does not break out with wild impetuousness on any one single occasion, but is always there, at any time and in the heart of every German, whether it is triggered off by something in particular that fills his heart with pride, or whether he gathers together with hundreds of thousands of other fellow countrymen to listen to the Fuhrer- or whether there is no external reason at all and it man-ifests itself in a moment of quiet reflection during the course of his daily work. Whenever anyone thinks of the Fuhrer, there is always a deep love which rises within him and of itself justifies the statement: "Hitler is Germany - Germany is Hitler." Never before has any man been closer to the heart of every German as this man, who himself came from their midst. He did not come from outside, but was born in the cradle of the nation, having felt its sorrow and lived its life, and if anyone today were to ask the name of the unknown German soldier at the front, then the whole of the German nation would answer: Adolf Hitler.

He was the conscience of the nation, from him came the cry of suffering and also of de-fiance of an oppressed people, in him the will to live of the whole of Germany at the hour of its greatest humiliation became word and deed. Adolf Hitler never once uttered a single word than those which the people thought in the depths of their souls, never once committed an act than those which the entire country would have wanted. He was never, is and will never be a dictator who imposes his personal opinions and his desire for power on the people. He is really only a Fuhrer (leader, guide, head), which is the greatest thing that can be said of a man. This is

During a trip through East Prussia the Fuhrer visited a peasant family.

18

On the day of the reintegration of the Saar.

Enthusiastic crowds in the presence of the Fuhrer in the
port of Hamburg.

Delegation from the Saar in front of the Imperial Chancellory.

She wants the hand of the Fuhrer.

Everyone wants to shake the Fuhrer's hand just once.

Even the peasants believe in the Fuhrer.

The Fuhrer's eyes — Father's eyes.

why he is so beloved by the people, this is why he is so trusted, this is why his people are so unspeakably happy. For the first time in its history the German people have become themselves.

Herein lies the secret of the indestructibility of Adolf Hitler and of his work, the assurance of the irrevocability of the path he has adopted, because he is no longer the man Adolf Hitler, it is no longer his work, no longer his path, but it is the German people themselves who express themself through him. In him the Germans love themselves, in him they follow their most secret wishes, in him their boldest thoughts become reality. Every single person feels this, and for that reason Adolf Hitler is a stranger to no one and no one is a stranger to the Fuhrer. Workers and peasants, Nobel prize winners and artists, soldiers and dreamers, the happy and the desperate, speak to him, and everyone hears his own language, understands and is understood. Everything is done without design and in a completely natural way, and no one stands in awe of the great man. No one is ordered about, no one is courted, but everyone is called on as he was called on by his own conscience, and he can do nothing but follow if he does not want to feel guilty and unhappy in his own mind. So what must happen happens of its own will, and no people on earth are freer than the German people.

Thus the German people do not tire of listening to the words of the Fuhrer, and if the party conference of the Reich in Nuremberg were to last twice as long, the people would still stand there on the last day as they did on the first and listen. He could drive through Germany continually, the people would wait day after day beside the road as they did on the first day and cheer him on, bringing him their children so that he could gaze at Germany's future. If they had to, they would also give him their lives as hundreds of his party members did in the years of fighting.

There have been emperors and kings, sovereigns and folk heroes, upsurgers and men of terror, clever and great rulers at the head of nations, but never before has there been a man like the Fuhrer. This is unique and is the great fortune which has been given to the German people. As long as one does not appreciate this, one cannot appreciate anything about the German people, one cannot understand why their eyes light up, their voices cheer, their arms fly up, their hearts beat faster when Adolf Hitler appears before the German people. And from these external signs which show the constant and mysterious attachment between the people and the Fuhrer, Hitler again draws strength for new works, just as the people draw strength from his sight.

This is seen particularly when the youth of Germany and the Fuhrer come face to face, and whoever has spent some time with the Fuhrer and been able to accompany him in these days, weeks and months, will have a store of unforgettable pictures.

Between Stettin and Pasewalk, a distance of at least ten kilometres, young Germans had taken up their positions in the middle of the country road in the rain and storm, because they had heard from someone somewhere that the Fuhrer would pass this way today. Evening was falling, and when the Fuhrer's car with its two escort cars roared along the road, far ahead in the distance between the trees lining the road, a crowd could be seen. As the cars drew nearer a throng of flagwaving children came into view. They were burning red, blue and green Bengal matches, and a number of children were standing guard before the bulk of the group to indicate by their waving hands that the convoy was to stop. Even though time was incredibly short, the Fuhrer still gave the order to stop, and at that moment the cars were surrounded by about a hundred children who jumped not only onto the running boards but even crept onto the radiators and bonnets in an attempt to catch a glimpse of the Fuhrer inside the car through the windscreens.

After the three cars in the convoy had been thoroughly inspected in this way, a particularly resourceful lad finally caught sight of the Fuhrer. He screamed at the top of his voice: "He's here, everyone over here!" - and then everything happened. The escort command had to step in because a number of boys were even trying to climb onto the swaying canvas hood of the car. The leader of the young troup, the same young boy who had discovered the Fuhrer, held a short speech, young, fresh and carefree, and then everyone made way for a young girl dressed in white. The girl curtsied deeply and then recited a poem she had composed herself about the joy young people had in seeing the Fuhrer. When she finished the child handed Adolf Hitler a small basket of rosy red apples.

Deeply moved, the Fuhrer stroked her blond hair, upon which the child suddenly burst into tears of overflowing joy and happiness. Slowly the convoy then moved away from the host of children, and for a long time the flag waving little figures could be seen through the rear windows of the cars bidding their farewells.

At every rally it is always the children who stand in the front rows. The well-behaved and unassuming ones stand there just as their teacher or troup leader has placed them, in straight rows and not moving from their spots. The more bold ones among them, however, hang in the trees, sit on memorials and the ledges of buildings, or stand like an avenue of living statues on top of tall factory walls, perch on flag poles and lantern poles, and, wherever the Fuhrer passes, fill the air with their endless cries of joy. The favourite places where children await the Fuhrer have always been sharp bends in the road. By their clever positioning they render these bends even sharper and force the cars to drive as slowly as possible. Better still if one comes upon a construction site somewhere on a country road. Here it is quite certain that the Fuhrer will only be able to proceed at a very slow pace and the opportunity to capture him will definitely present itself. It then inevitably becomes a real effort to extricate oneself from the crowd. When finally a path opens up in front of the cars, the children will run from behind the car only to block the way again with their joyous cheers.

Old people trust the Fuhrer.

A photo of the election campaign in Hessen in 1932.

Once in a town in the south of Germany, on the evening of a rally for the Fuhrer, tens of thousands of Hitler youth formed a guard of honour in the streets. The further the line extended, the tighter the two walls of the guard of honour were pushed together, so that finally there remained just enough room for the car to squeeze through. At first everything went well. Suddenly, however, there was much running, pushing and shoving, and while initially the torchlight bearers standing in the front row managed to contain the crowd they were suddenly carried along and pushed towards the cars. Their torches shone into the insides of the cars, and in their enthusiasm and love, they gave the Fuhrer and his entourage a heavy portion of smoke to inhale. It was fortunate that they did not set fire to the cars themselves. Only after a quarter of an hour did the Fuhrer succeed in extricating himself again from this enthusiastic crowd of young people.

It is amusing to see the seriousness and eagerness with which the young people endeavour to photograph the Fuhrer. They stand there with their tiny cameras, shaking with nervousness and excitement, their finger on the button. From the sight of these cameras you would think that it would only be sheer luck if a photo were to succeed. And yet it is just among these snapshots that you find a surprisingly large number of good photos. Here also luck seems to be on the side of the young people, because, on the other hand, experienced amateur photographers often complain that it is impossible for them to seize a favourable opportunity in the general excitement and massive crowds of people.

Elections in Frankfurt — 1932.

On a trip through Upper Silesia the Fuhrer is greeted and a young girl has the honour of presenting him with a bouquet of flowers. She is also supposed to say a little poem as she hands him the flowers. She recites the first line without faltering, but then loses the thread due to her excitement. After looking around helplessly several times, she suddenly takes the flowers and, standing on the tips of her toes, she reaches towards the Fuhrer, presses the flowers into his hands and says "Hitler, here you are, I've forgotten everything!", whereupon she runs away.

There is a street. It is closed off and people are standing closely packed together. They are waiting and waiting. Many have been waiting for hours. They are waiting for the Fuhrer. They want to see him. Everyone wants to see him - men, women, boys and girls. "It is like a holiday today," says an old woman, and she is right, because the Fuhrer is coming to this little town for the first time.

From the roofs and gables of the houses flags are waving and garlands have been stretched above the streets. The whole town has put on its festive dress. And then the Fuhrer arrives . . . A whirlwind seems to rush through the crowd. Here and there the orderly rows begin to bulge, the people push and jostle each other, arms are raised towards the Fuhrer, laughter and sobs are heard, all expressions of the joy and enthusiasm these people have for their Fuhrer. The women lift their children onto their arms and their little arms jut out above the heads of the crowds. Their eyes beaming and their lips smiling, they add their voices to the enthusiastic "Heil Hitler'"'s of the crowd.

The women and mothers gaze at the Fuhrer, trust and belief in their eyes. They know that it is only him whom they have to thank for the fact that their unemployed men have found work again, and can feed their families. Life once again has a purpose, and without fear and worrying they can once again look towards the future.

There is a letter which a young girl doing her year's service in the country wrote to her parents: " . . . I must start to write another page. I am sure that what I am about to write to you now will make you very happy. Can you believe it, my dear parents, I have seen the Fuhrer! Just imagine, the Fuhrer!! . . ."

What emotion was conveyed by these four words: "Just imagine, the Fuhrer!". The pride in her experience and the immensity of the love of this child of the German people for her Fuhrer are astonishing! It is the fullfilment of a wish which this child probably never had the courage to harbour. It is a genuine present of fate which in the middle of her year of country

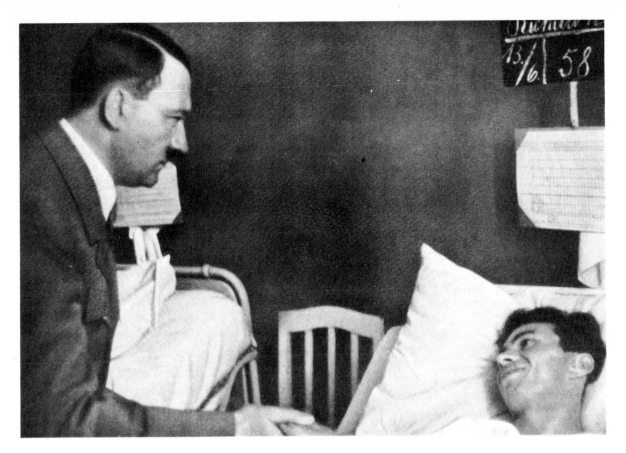

A visit to the victims of Reinsdorf.

service afforded her the most beautiful thing there is - a meeting with the Fuhrer. "Just imagine, what that means . . .!"

And it is like this everywhere, in Bavaria and in East Prussia, in Silesia and in the Rhineland.

On a country road in the Palatinate two men from the Arbeitsdienst* are marching towards the next town. The Arbeitsdienst camp lies a long way off in the country, and it is a long way to the railway station. But the two men are in high spirits and are whistling, becuase they are going home on holidays after months of healthy and strenuous work. They whistle: "In der Heimat, in der Heimat**... . . " Just then a line of cars sweeps past the two men. "They're lucky", one of them says. "They'll be there sooner than we will," the other says. "They're waving!" both call out together. And then, in fact, the line of cars comes to a halt and waits until the two men, who have begun to run, have caught up. "Where from? Where to? Climb in!" The two men open their eyes wide in amazement, because the man stopping in the middle of the country road and inviting them to climb in is none other than the Fuhrer. He makes them describe for him their lives and asks to know in great detail what it is like in their labour camp. In no time they arrive at the little town. The cars stop. As they leave the Fuhrer asks one of the two men: "It is about to rain. Don't you have a coat with you?" "I have no civilian coat, my Fuhrer. I was unemployed for a long time." On hearing this the Fuhrer takes off his grey travelling coat and hangs it on the shoulders of his fellow countryman. And before the latter can utter a work of thanks, the line of cars is already speeding away.

Somewhere a group of young workers in a large factory have lined up for roll call. The

*   Arbeitsdienst — NS Labour Service
**   Heimat — homeland (A favourite word to refer to Germany at the time.'

Fuhrer inspects the rows and looks deeply into the eyes of each of the young men. He turns to one of the young workers: "Are you a member of the Party?" - "No!" - "Are you one of the SA*?" — "No, I belong to the workers." — "Where were you before?" the Fuhrer asks after a short interval. The blond young man lowers his head, and then raises it and says, haltingly: "I was a young Communist, my Fuhrer!" He is obviously finding it difficult to speak. All eyes are turned towards him. An embarrassing moment. Then the Fuhrer takes the young man's hand, presses it, and says, smiling: "But today you are all with me, my young man." And, blushing deeply, the young man replies: "In the name of God, you can be sure of that, my Fuhrer!"

In this way, picture is heaped upon picture of the solidarity of every individual of the German people with Adolf Hitler.

In Hamburg on the occasion of the Fuhrer's rally on the eve of a decisive public opinion poll, a seriously disabled ex-serviceman pushes his way with his son through the safety chains which sealed off the access to the Fuhrer's quarters with the words: "I want to serenade the Fuhrer." The SS men let the man pass, and he took up his position on the street under the Fuhrer's window. With trembling fingers he removed his instrument from his grey cloak and played a song. The crowd of many thousands maintained a reverent silence. Plaintively the tunes of the street musician sought out the ear of the Fuhrer. And the Fuhrer heard the music. The Fuhrer had the man come to him, spoke with him and listened to the story of his life. "I have been unemployed for four years now," the disabled man's concluding words were. "My Fuhrer , can't you help me find a livelihood again?" The Fuhrer waved to one of his adjutants. Two rapid telepone calls ensued, and then the Fuhrer said: "Report tomorrow to this place. You can start work there immediately." In a flash the news spread amongst the waiting crowd. A seemingly unending, stormy ovation roared up to the Fuhrer by way of thanks.

Unforgettable also is the day when the Fuhrer appeared at the funeral of the victims of explosion catastrophe in Reinsdorf. The coffins of the fallen work heroes stood in long rows. The flags were flying at half mast, decked in dark crepe. The mourners stood by in silence. In one particular area the next of kin of the dead men had gathered together. It was a picture of boundless sorrow to see the weeping mothers, sisters, brothers and fathers. Then the Fuhrer appeared and the funeral oration began. The suffering of the relatives was heartbreaking. The orators and ministers spoke, the song of the good comrade was heard, and the final salutes boomed over the field. Then the Fuhrer left his entourage and walked unaccompanied over to the relatives. Hundreds of arms reached out towards him seeking comfort, and all those who were present will always remember the anguished face of the Fuhrer as he now stood in the midst of this deeply sorrowful gathering. Then he began to speak to or silently take the hands of the men and women in turn. The circle around him grew tighter and tighter. Tears died up and people who had broken down in their sorrow straightened up again. Now the Fuhrer took the head of an inconsolable old woman who had lost her son in his comforting hands, now he helped up with a few kindly words a deathly pale Hilter youth whose father was one of the fallen. So strong was the comfort which the Fuhrer gave to the mourners, because they were not alone in their sorrow. When the relatives then raised their arms in farewell and thanked Adolf Hitler once again silently, the Fuhrer and his people were so infinitely close, even in this hour of deepest distress.

*SA — Sturmabteilung — NS Storm Troopers.

The Fuhrer and the German people . . . Once there was a rally in the festival hall in Frankfurt, and while the Fuhrer was addressing the thousands inside, a woman stole her way to his car and placed a tiny bunch of lily of the valley — it was mid-winter — on the seat in which, in her estimation, the Fuhrer would sit after the rally. When the line of cars sped off after the conclusion of the gathering, a clear, penetrating voice was heard above the roaring cheers: "The lily of the valley is from me!"

Saar Rally on the Ehrenbreitstein in August 1934.

Hundreds and thousands of such moving and humourous, stirring and amusing stories could still be told. All of them, however say only the one thing, namely that a miracle has occurred, such as happens to a people only once in its history, that here the Fuhrer and his people are one and the same, and that the love which binds the people with their Fuhrer is so great, so spontaneous, so self-evident and joyous, that it breaks forth at every minute in renewed form, but always with the same intensity.

What an unending strength and what an unending blessing blossoms forth from this love for both the people and the Fuhrer, for the Fuhrer and the German people.

Minister Darre greets the Fuhrer on the occasion of the harvest festival.

28

Adolf Hitler

Congress of the German
worker's Front.

9th November, 1934, in Munich. In front of the Feldherrnhalle
Hitler speaks to members of the Hitler Jugend and the Bundes
Deutscher Madel who have just been admitted into the Party.

(Hitler Jugend = Hitler Youth. Bundes Deutscher
Madel = female counterpart to Hitler Youth)

The Fuhrer as an Orator
by Dr Joseph Goebbels

There are two types of orators which differ fundamentally and essentially: those who speak from the head or the intellect, and those who speak from the heart. Accordingly they also turn to two types of people: those who listen with their intellect, and those who listen with their heart. Orators of the intellect are generally produced by the parliament; orators of the heart are born of the people.

For the orator of the intellect it is imperative that he have at his disposal a wealth of statistics and knowledge, if he is to speak effectively. he must master dialectics as the pianist masters the keyboard. With the icy coldness of a relentlessly developed logic he orders his chain of thoughts and draws from them his inevitable conclusions. He is effective mainly with people who are accustomed to working principally or exclusively with their intellect. Great, rousing successes are denied him. He is unable to stir the masses to the depths of their souls, nor can he rouse them to achieve great and monumental goals. He remains limited to the purely didactic.

The Fuhrer with Reichsarbeitsfuhrer Hierl addressing
47,000 workers at the Reichsparteitag in 1935.

(Reichsparteitag = party conference of the Reich)

As he himself is cold, so he leaves those around him cold. At best he is able to sway people, but he can never rouse the masses and mobilise them, regardless of their own advantage or even to the acceptance of death and danger.

It is different with the orator who speaks from the heart. That is not to say that he has no control over the skills of which the orator of the intellect is the master. Frequently they serve him only as tools which he, as a true virtuoso of rhetoric, uses at his discretion. In addition to this, however, he has other capabilities which the intellectual orator can never hope to attain: the clarity of his diction combines with the seemingly natural simplicity of his train of thoughts; he divines instinctively what must be said and how it must be said. He united the greatness of the poetic spectacle with the monumental nature of the ideas he expounds. He knows the most secret hopes and aspirations of the soul of the masses, and knows how to reveal and stir them as if by a masterstroke. His speeches are masterpieces of declamation. In a far-reaching epic form he portrays people and circumstances; with a sharp stylus he engraves his theories on the slates of time; with elevated and noble emotion the looming pillars of his philosophy tower over his chain of thoughts. Just as his voice speaks from the depths of his being, so does it penetrate deep into the listener's being. It causes the most secret strings of the human soul to resound. It stirs the indolent and the lazy, it rouses the half-hearted and the doubtful, cowards it turns into men and weaklings into heroes.

Such words are only rarely heard by history. However, once they penetrate a lethargic period with their omnipotence, then people and circumstances are orientated anew by them.

These rhetoric geniuses are the drum beaters of destiny. They begin as loners in degenerate and crumbling periods of history and suddenly and unexpectedly stand in the middle of the brightest spotlights of a new evolution. These are orators who shape the history of a people.

Like every great man, the orator of renown also has his own style. He can only speak as he is. His words are an integral part of him. Whether on an appeal, on a poster, in a letter or an essay, during an address or a speech, he speaks the language which corresponds to his nature and his manner.

There are numerous examples in history which demonstrate perfectly that eminent orators resemble each other only in greatness of their desired effect. The manner of their call to the people and their appeal to the hearts, on the other hand, is always essentially different and varies according to the time, the nation and the character of the era. Caesar spoke differently to his legions than Frederick the Great to his infantrymen, and Napoleon spoke differently to his guards than Bismarck to the representatives of the Prussian state parliament. And yet each of them used the language which the people they were dealing with understood, and used words and thoughts which kindled enthusiasm in their minds and met with a response in their hearts. They gave a concrete expression to the deepest and most puzzling demon of their time, and in doing so have been handed down in history as the harbingers of the great ideas of the time who made history and formed the lives of peoples.

It also seems as if different races vary in their disposition to the powers of oratory, as if there are people whose talents are not suited to this rousing art, and then again others who seem almost destined for it. It is not in vain that one speaks of a Latin eloquence. The plentitude of indifferent and important talents as far as rhetoric is concerned in the Romans gives this a certain justification. And it is also probably true to add that these talents for rhetoric were directed at a public which understood it, fostered it and gave orators the greatest possibe opportunities to exercise their talents.

Speech to the staff of Blohm & Voss.

Taking over the Reichsfuhrerschule in Bernau in 1933.   (school for the leaders of the Reich)

The Fuhrer views the
Motorised Troops.

Adolf Hiter in the
Landsberg Fortress.

The Fuhrer in the election campaign for Germany's
freedom. March, 1936.

As far as oratory is concerned, the German people have not been served well in the past. They have brought forth in abundance statesmen and soldiers, musicians and poets, architects and engineers, expert planners and organisers. But there has always been a shortage of great rhetoric talents. Since Fichte addressed the German nation with his classical speeches, there has been no one who stirred the hearts of the people,until Bismarck's call to his time. When Bismarck left the rostrum it remained empty of real talent, until a new harbinger of the peoples' suffering arouse out of the collapse after the Great War. What existed between these times was at best mediocre, sufficing the daily business of parliament and sittings of the board, but meeting only with an icy reserve as far as the people, who should have been deeply roused, were concerned.

This may have been a product of the times themselves. There were no great ideas and no idealistic projects; times were barren and sated. The only illusory revolt at the time, Marxism, was secretly aligned to the time, and its supporters were representatives of materialism, which has never ignited the spark of true geniuses.

Revolutions, however, give birth to true orators, and true orators give rise to revolutions. In the course of a revolution one must not overestimate the written or printed word; it is the spoken word which arouses the hearts and minds of people with the secret magic of its immediate effect. People perceive with their eyes and ears, and the infectious force of the masses who are gripped by the sound of the human voice carries along irresistibly in its spell those who are still wavering and doubting.

Where would the statesman of genius, who has sown the seeds of a higher and unfathomable destiny, be if he did not have at his disposal the strength of speech and the explosive power of words! It gives him the possibility to make ideas from ideals, and reality from ideas. With its help he gathers around his flag people who are prepared to fight for it; driven by it men risk their lives and livelihood to lead a new world to victory. From the propaganda of the word organisations are formed, from the organisation the movement develops, and the movement conquers the state. It is not a question of whether the ideas are correct; what is crucial is that they are

**The Fuhrer opens the party conference on freedom (1935)
in the historic town hall auditorium in Nuremburg.**

correctly presently to the masses, and that the masses themselves become their propagators. Theories will always remain theories if men do not carry them out. In times of turmoil, however, men obey only one appeal which ignites in their hearts because it comes from the heart.

It is difficult to classify the Fuhrer in this series. His skill in moulding the masses is so amazing and unique that no pattern or dogma can be superimposed upon it. It would be absurd to think that he had ever attended a school for oratory or speech; he is a genius of rhetoric. His rhetoric is unique to him and has never been influenced by anyone else. One could never imagine that the Fuhrer had ever spoken differently than he now speaks, or that he will ever speak differently. He says what comes from his heart, and his words therefore go straight to the heart of his listeners. He possesses the remarkable gift of instinctively sensing what is in the air. He has the ability of expressing it so clearly, logically and unreservedly that the listener comes to believe that what is being expounded has always been his own opinion. This is the actual secret of the magical effect of a Hitler speech. For the Fuhrer is neither exclusively a speaker from the intellect nor from the heart. He speaks from both according to the demands of the hour at hand. The essential characteristics of his speeches to the people are: clarity of structure, a relentlessly logical development of his chain of thoughts, simplicity and general intelligibility of expression, razor-sharp dialectics, a marked and never deceptive instinct for the masses and their feelings, a fascinating emotionalism which is used with the utmost economy, and the power of being able to appeal to the soul and generating an immediate response.

The orator... ...Adolf Hitler...

Once, many years ago when the Fuhrer was still a long way from power, he spoke to a gathering which consisted largely of political opponents. In the beginning he was therefore met with only icy rejection. In a two hour match with the unruliness of his audience he lay aside all their objections and arguments. In the end he was speaking to a sea of people shouting to the furthermost row: "Hitler is our Columbus!"

This summarizes the essence of Hitler's speech. Hitler had managed to inspire the people. The times and the longings of the people were confused and secretive, but he had clarified them and wrested from them their secrets. He showed them again to his listeners clearly and simply, in such a way as the man on the street had long perceived them but had never before had the courage to express them. Hitler said what everyone thought and felt! More than that: he had the courage of his convictions against the opposition of almost everyone present to draw a moral and to make demands with an iron logic which arose from the needs of the time.

The Fuhrer is the first person in the evolution of Germany who used language as a tool to fashion history. When he started he had nothing else. He began with only the strength of his mighty heart and the power of his mere words. With both he reached deeply into the souls of the people. He did not recognize the needs and worries which oppressed the little man and speak about them; but for him they were only a mere depiction, he was not a tendentious describer of the existing conditions like the others. He situated the difficulties of the day in their general national sense and gave them a meaning which reached further than the actual day. He appealed not to the bad, but to the good instincts of the masses. His speech was a magnet which drew the blood and iron that still existed in the people to it.

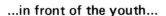 ...in front of the youth...

...Reichsparteitag 1935
(Party Conference of the Reich).

Stupid and arrogant bourgeois blockheads delighted for some time in saying that he was only beating his own drum. They were making fun of themselves, and did not know why. Because they themselves were so completely lacking in the power of oratory, they saw in it a lesser form of statesmanship. They were only after power, without fully understanding that Marxism had taken the power from them by force and would only ever return it to them by force. They formed conventions in which a people's movement was forced to march up. They tried their hand at coups where a revolution was in the air. They displayed contempt for the masses because they were unable to control the masses. For the masses surrender only to a man who can take them under his inexorable command. They obey only when someone understands how to give them orders. Their instincts are too acute not to be able to distinguish whether something is really meant or merely said.

This is perhaps the classic proof of the inner purity of the German people. They lent their ear to the appeal of a man who had only himself and his words to challenge the state and the society, the press and public opinion, and all that seemed sensible and useful. And this is also on the other hand the classic proof of the rhetoric genius of the Fuhrer which towers above all times. His word alone caused a whole era to totter, a seemingly established state to collapse and a new era to dawn.

**Courtyard of Braunschweig
Castle, 1931.**

Braunschweig, 1931.

A historical orator who triggers off such an effect must have at his disposal all the possibilities of the spoken word. And such is the case with the Fuhrer. He speaks to workers just as naturally and supremely well as he does to scientists. His words penetrate just as deeply into the hearts of the farmers as the city dwellers. When he speaks with children they feel deeply touched by his words. When he speaks with men, the magic of his voice stirs their most secret feelings. His speeches are the philosophy of history translated into the language of the people. He has the gift of calling forth long forgotten great historical epochs from the past and presenting them in such a way that they seem well known even to those who had never known them or heard about them. His speeches are totally devoid of the provocative tone of one-upmanship which usually characterises the so-called speeches of scholarly men.

Again and again his words revolve around the central thought of the people and developing nation of our race. His wording to express this are without measure. The listener never has the feeling that he has heard it all before. The people are continually impressed anew and in ever changing ways with the great and fundamental thought of our national rebirth. At the same time this type of rhetoric is devoid of anything doctrinaire. If a fact sounds initially like an assertion, it is inevitably verified in the course of his explanation by an inexhaustible abundance of examples. These examples are not taken from one particular section of the population and society, with the result that other sections remain unconvinced of their power of proof. They all come from the knowledge that this speaker, contrary to all the parliamentary charlatans, believes what he says.

In his speeches the mundane side of life comes alive and holds the listener captive. Here the sufferings of the day are tackled not only with the heavy-handed tools of philosophy, but with wit and the sting of irony. Here humour manifests both tears and laughter and celebrates its triumphs. Here a note is struck which also resounds through the sorrows and worries of everyday life.

An unmistakeable sign that a speech meets the highest standards is the fact that it not only sounds good, but also reads well. The speeches of the Fuhrer are stylistic masterpieces, whether

Germany's youth.

Flowers for the Fuhrer.

they be totally impromptu, or developed along the lines of a few brief key-words, or read from carefully formulated notes on the occasion of an important international gathering. Those not in his immediate vicinity can scarcely distinguish whether the written speech is being made freely, or whether the speech being made freely is the result of a carefully worded written speech. Because both are polished speeches in the best sense of the word. This picture would not be complete it if were not mentioned that the Fuhrer is an outstanding creator and master of public debate. The last time a large section of the general public had the opportunity of seeing him as such was during his clash with the social democrats at the Reichstag of 1933, when he responded to a clumsy and insolent complaint made by Wels, a member of the Reichstage at the time. People had the feeling that a game of cat and mouse was taking place. Marxism was driven from one corner to another, and where it hoped for mercy, it was met only with annihilation. With an almost breathtaking precision his rhetoric lashes pelted him. Without the aid of a script or any hastily sketched keywords the Fuhrer held his great, long-awaited reckoning with those social democrats who were old hands in parliament and who now received the coup de grace. How often before had he pushed them into a corner in his meeting whenever they dared to approach him.

At that time they still had the opportunity of falsely reporting humiliating defeats as triumphant victories in their newspapers. Now, before the eyes of all the people, they succumbed to his power and were threatened with complete defeat.

All those judges and public prosecutors who had wanted to take Hilter for a ride, when he appeared as a witness or a defendant, with their seemingly naive and harmless questions or their stupid and dull comments, have a tale or two to tell about this relentless, rhetoric mind on the offensive. A triumphant victory for the defendants arose from the People's Court Trial of 1924, which was supposed to resolve judicially the rebellion of the 8th and 9th of November 1923, because the Fuhrer countered the mountains of lies, malice and lack of understanding with the radiant strength of his open truthfulness and the compelling effect of his forceful eloquence. And it is not without regret that the Republic took note of the Army Trial in Leipzig in 1930, which was supposed to destroy the Fuhrer and his movement, but which in reality served as a springboard for his rhetorical effectiveness which spread into the rest of the world. One can only recall with horror the fact that a Jewish Communist lawyer could once call him as a witness before a Berlin court and bombard him with questions for nine hours without a break, and note with proud satisfaction that here Jewish bolshevism was opposed by a man who relentlessly cut him short with the power of his oratory and did not desist until he lay overwhelmed on the floor.

We saw and experienced the Fuhrer as an orator in the Party Conference of Freedom in 1935. He spoke to the masses fifteen times in the space of seven days. In doing so, not once did he repeat the same thought or use the same turns of phrase. Each time what he said sounded fresh, young, vital and insistent. He spoke differently to the office workers than to the SA and the SS, and he spoke differently to the youth than he did to the women. He, who in his great talk on culture, bared the most secret secrets of artistic creation, addressed himself in his speech to the army to the last soldier in the last batallion, and was understood by him. He has cast an arc under which the life of the whole German people takes place. He has become a messenger of the word who approaches his manifold existence with the divine grace of language.

The Fuhrer is at his very best as an orator when he speaks in a very small circle. Here he continually addresses himself to every single one of his listeners. This gives his talk the impression of a moving stream which continues without a moment's rest and arouses in the listener the sort of interest which never wanes, because the listener continually feels he is being personally spoken to. It may be that he is speaking on a topic that has been raised purely by chance and to which he lends an expertise which strikes everyone and causes the specialist to marvel at his knowledge, or it may be that an everyday matter is mentioned incidentally by someone and is suddenly bestowed with fundamental universality.

The Fuhrer speaks to the German people.

Here the Fuhrer touches on the heart of matters more intimately and in greater detail than his public speechs permit in order to lay it bare with a relentless logic. Only someone who has heard him speaking face to face like this can grasp the immensity of his rhetoric genius.

Of his speeches to his people and to the world one can in fact say that they are words which strike an audience such as history has never before seen. They are also words which ignite in the heart and which continue to have a lasting effect on the formation of a new international epoch. There is probably scarcely one man today in the whole of the civilised world who has not once heard the sound of his voice, whether he understood his words or not, and in whose heart of hearts the magic of his voice has not met with a response. Our people can consider themselves lucky to know that there is a voice above them to which the world listens, a voice which is blessed with the ability of turning words into thoughts and setting an era into motion with these thoughts. This man belongs to those people who have the courage of saying yes and no without subsequently modifying what they have said by an if or a but. In a situation where, in every country of the world, millions and millions of people have been hit by bitter suffering, grave afflictions and terrible sorrow, in which there is hardly one star in the dark clouds that hang over the skies of Europe, in which people are filled and driven by dulled longings which they lack the gift and grace of expressing, he stands over Germany as one amongst the uncounted millions silent in their torture who whom God has given the ability to say what we suffer!

Dr Goebbels

39

A walk on the Obersalzberg (mountain in the south of Germany).

The Fuhrer in his Private Life
by Obergruppenfuhrer Wilhelm Bruckner

It goes without saying that a man who is as entrenched in his political work as the Fuhrer must sacrifice his private life to his work. And if ever he wants to free himself from the pressures of his official duties, the problems associated with politics nevertheless follow him to the furthest corners of the German homeland, whether it be a small, quiet village in the dunes near the Baltic Sea or Haus Wachenfeld on the Obersalzberg. They pursue him not only in the form of telephone calls and telegrams, letters and files. He can never banish from his heart the constant political work, his concern for Germany. It is with this concern uppermost in his mind that the Fuhrer goes to bed late at night and awakes early in the morning. He is pursued by the difficulties concerning foreign affairs, the necessities of the new employment onslaught, difficulties in the domain of financial policy, necessities of assuring the well-being of the German people, problems of youth education, questions about German culture, decisions within the framework of the restoration of German military security, and so it goes unendingly. There is scarcely a conversation which does not lead immediately to the central political issues, scarcely an experience which does not at once recall important decisions. After all, everything in Germany begins with this man and ends with him. And if he seems to be relaxing for a few days in total seclusion, then he is probably only preparing himself for new and weighty decisions to be met or for a new intensive work output. Indeed, even in his aeroplane he is met by radio telegrams from his Reichsleiter* and ministers.

Thus the private life of the Fuhrer is merged with his public life and his work for Germany. If one wants to talk about his private life, all that can actually be said is that it consists of transferring his political work from the offices of the Chancellery to less official rooms.

* leaders of the Reich

On the Obersalzberg. A neighbour greets the Fuhrer.

In an aeroplane.

He is allowed to look through the telescope.

41

Prime Minister Goring at the Fuhrer's place on the Obersalzberg.

A comrade from the field visits the Fuhrer.

Despite all this he finds time to concern himself with all aspects of art and science. His favourite relaxation after a stressful day's work is to listen to an opera or a symphony concert. Only then is he completely removed from the pressing issues of the day, and many a great, creative thought has arisen from his absorption in the powerful realm of music.

Even in the rooms of his official residence in the Chancellery the Fuhrer welcomes from time to time leading German artists who bring him the best creations of our time. On many occasions after the artistic performances the conversations about music and drama, poetry and novels, architecture and philosophy, continue on until late at night. There are few people who have not left his house stimulated and inspired after such an evening.

Besides music, the theatre and architecture, the Fuhrer is particularly interested in film,

Haus Wachenfeld on the Obersalzberg near Berchtesgaden.

An encounter on the Obersalzberg.

as it is the most recent branch of creative art. Film equipment in the Great Hall of the Chancellery enables the Fuhrer to see what is being produced by Germany and the rest of the world, between the pressing issues of the day. From his own knowledge of matters the Fuhrer has also stimulated many film producers in their work.

Often the Fuhrer invites to lunch visitors who have come to him for official talks. so that he can find the time to discuss with them in greater detail any issue which has come to his notice in the course of the talk. Thus there will frequently be at his luncheon table people from the most diverse work and interest groups, officers and scientists, men from the world of business and the world of art, senior party officials and old fighting companions from the war and the early days of the movement. These people receive new information and inspiration not only from the Fuhrer, but also from each other in the course of their conversation.

The Fuhrer likes to use his weekends to see himself the morale of the people and to inform himself about the progress in the reconstruction work without taking part in an official tour. Then he drives throught the gaus* of Germany in the car he had come to love in the time of his struggles and at almost every spot some memory from the time of his rise to power comes alive. For his entourage it is always a renewed and deeply moving experience to witness the incredible love of the people with which the Fuhrer is met on such journeys.

There are a number of places in Germany to which the Fuhrer particularly likes to return for a short break. Above all, there is the house on the Obersalzberg which is known to all Germans and which is so closely linked with the history of the movement. On the Baltic Sea and the North Sea there are also a few places hidden among the dunes to which the Fuhrer likes to go for a short rest or to engage in important discussions.

* administrative areas under the NS

A walk in the mountains.

The Fuhrer and little Helga Goebbels.

Off duty.

44

Stew, also served for the Chancellor of the Reich.

The Fuhrer — beloved of the children.

Good news.

A Pimpf* hands the Fuhrer a letter from
his sick mother.

*Pimpf: member of Hitlerian organisation for 10-14 year olds.

A little visitor to the Fuhrer on the Obersalzberg.

On the G'schwandner Alm near Garnisch.

The Fuhrer during a summer vacation in front of the
Fruckerlehen near Berchtesgaden, where Dietrich
Eckart lived for some time in 1923.

Walks through the beech forests at sunset on the shores of a lake have often offered him a measure of relaxation and at the same time resulted in important political decisions. In the course of such walks children approach the Fuhrer freely, reach out to take his hand, chat with him and relate to him all their minor experiences which are nevertheless so important to them. Then it may happen that the Fuhrer takes time off from his most important discourses to devote himself entirely to the joys and sufferings of such a child.

In the larger seaports the navy gathers around the Fuhrer and accounts from the war, reports of submarine trips and the battles at Skagerrak enliven a short, relaxing evening. It is exactly like this in the small garrisons in the country where the Fuhrer often speaks in an exciting and impressive manner about his war experiences on the Western Front.

Often when he is travelling the Fuhrer will stop at a particularly charming spot in the country for a picnic, whether it be on a bright sunny day in summer or a beautiful, warm moonlit night. It then often happens that fruit pickers and wood gatherers suddenly pass by and stop in amazement when they realize that it is the Fuhrer they see here in a glade peeling an apple or eating a few sandwiches. He then waves to the hesitant onlookers and invites them to share in his meal.

Many people wonder why the Fuhrer has chosen the Obersalzberg of all places for his home. However, anyone who has ever stood up there realizes that there is probably no other place in Germany which, despite the mountains all around, offers such a far-reaching and unimpeded view of the beauty of the world. In a gap in the mountains to the north, at the foot of the Gaisberg, there nestles the old diocesan town of Salzburg. On days when the fohn* is blowing the castle

*fohn - Alpine wind

Evening on the Obersalzberg.

Four sturdy brothers.

One of the faithful.

The Joy of motherhood.

"My Fuhrer, may I present my grandchild."

and the little town can be seen with the naked eye. With the aid of a telescope all the details of the buildings can be seen even without the fohn which brings everything closer. To the left of the Obersalzberg there looms the massif of the Untersberg whose changing colours evoke a different atmosphere every day. Still further to the left the eye then wanders over to the Watzmann and the giant mountains which surround it and which finally appear to move closer in a wide arc and culminate in the Hoher Goll behind the Obersalzberg.

No day is like another here. At times the mists build up in the morning and stage a desperate battle with the sun high above them until they are defeated and forced to rise from the valleys, only to float as light white clouds against the azure sky around noon. At other times the day commences bright and sunny and every last detail of the landscape stands out sharply and clearly to the onlookers. The fohn descends warmly from the heights and fills the surrounding valleys with its mild, yearning atmosphere. At yet other times rain and snowstorms lash the mountains and the wind roars around the small, modest country house.

49

Hitler visits the Leadership
School in Munich.

Hitler visits the townspeople.

Here, amidst the magnificence of nature, which is a symbol of the human condition, the Fuhrer resides when he is preparing his great speeches, which have given a new impetus or a new direction not only to events in Germany, but also to the political happenings in the world. Here the crucial discussions take place before the laws and statutes which will decisively affect centuries to come take shape.

A German American of the Steuben Society grasped the meaning of this little country house during a visit to his old homeland, and later expressed the following words: "We Germans from America didn't recognize the new Germany. We knew only the old Germany and saw

The Fuhrer in front of his Landhaus (country house) on the Obersalzberg.

**The Fuhrer speaks to a
wounded soldier.**

Old comrades.

it again in the new country when we visited the palaces and castles from times gone by. But now we have come to know this house and in it we experience an obvious example of the contrast of the Germany created by Adolf Hitler to the old Germany. We also know now from what inexhaustible well he draws the material for his speeches."

And it is true that here, far from the confusing bustle of everyday life, and guided by the indestructible splendour of the landscape, his searching mind finds the right paths for his people and the fatherland. But the Fuhrer cannot enjoy the magnificent beauty of nature like a holidaymaker who has left behind all his business cares. The moment he arrives on the Obersalzberg he is met with an imposing number of letters and files, telegrams and telephone calls, and with each mail delivery new piles of work arrive. Almost daily his minister and Reichsleiter (leaders of the Reich) telephone to ascertain the Fuhrer's opinion on some important and pressing matter. Often they arrive in person at Berchtesgaden to talk with the Fuhrer during his short period of relaxation. Issues concerning party matters which had had to be postponed due to important political decisions in Berlin, are settled here, and many books of aesthetic and political literature of domestic or foreign origin, which were waiting in vain to be read in the Chancellery, are studied by the Fuhrer here in peace. His entourage has long since gone to sleep. There is a magnificent and deep stillness and the Fuhrer reads - these are his most enjoyable hours. On the following morning, however, the telephone exchange reports dozens of appointments which have come in, files lie open expectant before him, and the mail mounts up. Indeed, this is the way it is: When the Fuhrer is on the Obersalzberg for the purpose of "relaxation", the post office and the exchange in Berchtesgaden have their busiest time. And even the Fuhrer's entourage have more than their fair share of work because thoughts arrive thick and fast and decisions are made in rapid succession.

Before the communal breakfast the Fuhrer has already read the newspapers. He works through the papers himself rather than being presented with prepared excerpts. Then his adjutants, press secretary and the remaining men from his entourage report briefly on what lies ahead for the day. Then everyone sits down for breakfast, and immediately afterwards he takes care of his appointments - visitors, Reichsleiter, ministers, close co-workers and party members. In the meantime the mail is prepared and then presented to the Fuhrer, who sketches out brief answers or dictates them at once himself. And so the morning passes rapidly.

Welcome guests on the Obersalzberg are always his old comrades-in-arms: *Pg. Goring, Pr. Dr. Goebbels, the Reich's treasurer Schwarz, the Minister Adolf Wagner, and also the Reich's War Minister and many others. (* Pg. parteigenosse — party member).

The busy morning is usually followed by a brief or not so brief midday walk, or a trip to the surrounding area. The Fuhrer takes particular delight in hiking, summer and winter, to the "Goll-Hausl", where once Dietrich Erkart lived, until death tore him from the Fuhrer's side.

51

By the Obersee near Berchtesgaden.

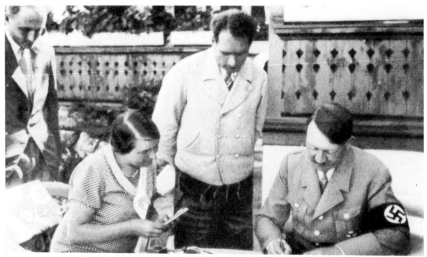

In the summer holidays on the Obersalzberg.

If the time is insufficient for an extended walk and work must be continued straight after lunch, then at least one brief hour will often be found during the afternoon coffee break to walk over to the little mountain inn on the Hochlenzer, or to visit the house of Prime Minister Goring, if its host is present. Then Pg. Goring likes to extend an invitation to an archery contest, of which he is a master.

Often, however, the Fuhrer has only a few brief moments in the day which he then spends in the garden of his house with his devoted Alsation dogs, or lost in thought in winter watching the birds sitting at the many feeding troughs and enjoying the seeds the Fuhrer has spread out for them in the morning. There is only one unshakeable daily occurrence. Every day hundreds and thousands of party comrades gather below on the drive to see the Fuhrer at the midday hour. The Fuhrer, who knows full well that they have all come to Berchtesgaden not only to see him, but to express to him the love of all the people, will allow nothing to deter him from granting their most ardent wish. Each time it is once again a most startling picture to see the joy which breaks forth when the Fuhrer walks down amongst them. Manual workers and professional workers alike have gathered here from all over Germany, and every day it is like another pilgrimage. Every one of them, the old and the young, walk past the Fuhrer. Their eyes light up, their hands rise in greeting and many of them are so seized by emotion that they have tears in their eyes. From the rows of people walking past can be heard cries which announce from which part of Germany they have come: "from East Prussia", "from Schleswig", "from Oldenburg", "from Saxony", "from Hamburg", and so forth. Young Pimpfs and BDM girls cannot be held back by the cordons. Quick as a flash they rush up to the Fuhrer, hand him their carefully prepared flowers and are overjoyed when the Fuhrer exchanges a few words with them. They are even more overjoyed when he invites a few of them to lunch or to afternoon coffee.

At mealtimes all his guests and co-workers sit harmoniously together, and often joyous laughter resounds through the room. These few moments are spent in a relaxed and peaceful manner. Frequently architects and artists visit and present their new plans to the Fuhrer. The Fuhrer takes pleasure in all aspects of the reconstruction of culture and discusses at length the plans brought to him. Dr. Todt, the Inspector General for the Reich's Autobahns, will also always receive the Fuhrer's full attention for his plans and photographs. The Fuhrer's old comrades-in-arms from the time of the World War are also always welcome guests on the Oberslazberg.

If at times it seems that the work on the Obersalzberg will never come to an end, the Fuhrer will then take a short, bracing walk to give him new vigour, and it is immaterial to him whether the hot summer sun is beating down, or crisp snow is covering the mountains, or rain is pelting down or mists are obscuring the visibility. These walks are not always sheer pleasure for his entourage, who, in the cities have grown out of the habit of mountain climbing. The Fuhrer walks very quickly, and even fit people often find it difficult to keep pace with him. Consequently many adjutants often have problems keeping up the tempo. While they are already exhausted and out of breath, the Fuhrer continues briskly and effortlessly.

These days of relaxation are short, and most of the time they are shortened even further by unexpected events. But what is certain is that nowhere does the Fuhrer find a lifestyle so suited to him as in the few days which he spends here on the mountain.

Just as in the course of thousands of years the mountains remain eternal, so will the work the Fuhrer has begun here live on eternally in his people for thousands of years to come.

New Year's Reception for the Diplomatic Corps, 1934.

The Fuhrer as a Statesman

by Dr Joseph Goebbels

All human greatness has its origin in the blood. Instinct is its guide and intuition its great saving grace. Intellect only ever contributes partially to the works of true genius; it is more concerned with checking the direction and meaning of these works and revealing them later to the eye of the beholder. These laws apply above all to art, the highest and most noble activity of men, which brings men closer to their divine origin. They apply in the same way to the dom— ain of great politics, which not in vain we call statesmanship, because such politics is in fact an art as it has all the essential characteristics of artistic creation. The sculptor puts his hammer and chisel to the cumbersome stone to imbue it with divine breath; the raw marble becomes an art— istic form. The painter uses the raw material of colour to recreate the noble picture of nature and reproduce it, as it were, a second time. The poet arranges the words of a basically formless language into a poem, a play or an epic portrayal, in which he depicts the human passions of good and evil.

The statesman has the raw material of the masses at his disposal. With the strength of his word and his work he moulds them into a living and breathing body of people; his brilliant plans show the people the goal of the nation. They are all created from the brilliant display which finally is an inspiration whose instrument the true artist considers himself to be. In addition there exists in all these domains the craftsmen, who also must have their place and whose duties and responsibilities are sharply delineated. They learn their work diligently and industriously and, if they belong to the better men in their occupation, acquire a wide and worthwhile knowledge of their craft, which they know how to use when required; but what they do remains an occupation and not a vocation. They are the talented in any artistic activity. The real artist, however, is a genius.

Herein lies the difference between talent and genius; talent creates from experience, from knowledge, and perhaps also from the imagination and the intellect, genius, on the other hand, from divine grace. Geniuses turn worlds upside down and erect new worlds. They are the great guides of peoples; the times align themselves to geniuses. They set the course history takes.

The saying that there is a child hidden inside every man applies particularly to the genius, because the genius acts from a childlike inhibitedness and approaches things with the confident lack of self-awareness with which children usually act.

The brilliant statesman dares the impossible to make what is possible possible. His actual strength lies in the simplification of seemingly irreconcilable differences. Before the average intellect has even seen or recognized the tasks waiting to be solved, the great Fuhrer has already come to grips with their solution.

Adolf Hitler, 2nd August 1914,
in Munich.

Visit to the Chancellory of the Reich (Prime Minister Gombos)

The problem urgently facing us Germans after the War consisted of shaping a uniformly thinking, feeling and acting nation from the conglomeration of states, parties, organisations and individuals. This problem did not initially come to light in the war; but the fact that it had not been solved finally cost us the war. For many centuries Germany had been excluded from world politics because of its internal disunity. We Germans have indulged our inner differences of opinion, whether they were of a religious, economic or social nature, and suffered terribly accordingly, while other nations, who recognized sooner than we did their destiny in world politics, begain to take over the world.

But it was not until the war that the continued impossibility of this situation was made clear. And yet, without learning from this terrible lesson, Germans did exactly the opposite of what history required of them. Never had particularism of every kind raged in Germany as in the time when we needed to rely most strongly on our internal unity.

In the years after the war it seemed at times as if Germany were finally about to leave the great interplay of world powers and withdraw into provincial isolation. All the prerequisites for standardizing the overall national mode of thinking were lacking; indeed, the so-called Weimar Constitution at the time, whose slurping beneficiaries were the parliamentary parties, represented to a certain extent the perpetuation of this internal disunity. The government withdrew itself from this task, turning its vigilance more within Germany rather than outside Germany. Its goal consisted of preserving and conserving the small remainder of internal freedom of movement and external sovereignty which had been left to us.

For a brilliant statesman who appeared at this time the first and most difficult test therefore consisted of recognizing the fact that within the Government itself the restitution of the inter—national standing of Germany was hopeless from the start and as a result should not even be attempted. Because the Government itself has surrendered this international standing by signing the Versailles Agreement, and had even gone a step further by jealously watching over the preservation of this document and considering any national movement against it as an attack on its own existence and punishing it accordingly.

The true statesman could therefore at that time not be found in the parties or the govern—ment, but outside the government. This government had to fall to make possible the process of the moral, social and economic restitution of the German people and, associated with this, the consolidation of a true government which would reflect his ideals. In the fight against the gov—ernment it therefore became a question of forming a government within the government in which all the laws could then be put to the test as far as the practical and organisational side of things were concerned. These laws would then later become the fundamental laws of the new govern—ment. The issue was not simply replacing the Weimar theory with a new theory, however well thought out and well meant it was. An association of men had to be gathered around the new theory to give this theory life, colour and real substance. The idea against the Weimar non—government had at its centre the necessity of a government, even in opposition, in the non—government, and of a people within the people who would embrace it. Only according to these principles could the process of regeneration of the German nation be put in motion.

Here began the statesmanlike work of the Fuhrer.

To begin with we must clarify a number of principal decisions which in a certain measure became the actual origins of his overall political actions. Already as an unknown corporal in the World War speaking in the turmoil of the revolution to Bavarian garrisons, the Fuhrer made a series of resolutions which point to the absolutely certain and sovereign instinct of the brilliant statesman, and which, through the very fact that at the time they were understood by scarcely anyone, later became the actual origin of his phenomenal and fantastic rise. They also provided the confirm—ation for the correctness of the philosophy which was taking shape in his head. It would have been easy for himsto join one of the existing parties. The attraction there was a quiet and assured livelihood and opportunities for promotion of all kinds. He could have soothed his tortured conscience with the notion that one had to save what could still be saved, and that therefore it seemed necessary to choose the lesser evil. He did none of this. He refused to do it because none of the existing parties offered the guarantee, let alone the possibility, of overcoming the spirit within Germany, and yet without the reunification of the German a solution to the nat—ional German problem in the statesmanlike sense was out of the question altogether. Here

An historic meeting. Eden and Simon with the Fuhrer.

already we see the instinctive sense of a gifted man who would rather take upon himself the seeming hopelessness of a desperate struggle starting with nothing against the government, the power of money, the press and the parties, than to burden the beginning of his work with a compromise.

It was the fashion of the time to go along with the government. There were two reasons for this: one was to identify with the government, the other was to attempt to reform the gov—ernment from within. The Fuhrer adhered to neither of the two, because he knew that this government was wrong in its conception and that it could not therefore be reformed but rather had to be sidestepped to enable the formation of a true government. Later on there were men and parties who, when they recognized or professed to recognize the impossibility of the reform of the Weimar system from within, began to take the lead in opposing the system from outside; but they had been burdened from the outset with the compromise of an albeit temporary peace treaty with the Weimar democracy. Only the Fuhrer could refer his opposition from the first to the last days to the fact that he had never made a pact with the parliamentary regime and therefore appeared to be the only one destined to give it its coup de grace in its final hour.

Parties and politicians at that time never spoke to the people as a nation; they only ever addressed individual parts of the nation. The worker parties spoke to the workers, the bourgeois parties to the middle classes, the denominational parties to their denominations and the farmer parties to the farmers. To the casual observer in the first meetings of the National Socialist Worker Party in Munich, where the Fuhrer addressed scarcely one hundred people, it may at times have appeared grotesque that the call nevertheless was always to the nation. He spoke neither to the educated nor to the proletariat and rejected buying the approval of the masses

57

through cheap flattery. Today one must go back to these origins of the National Socialist move—ment and the actual leadership of Adolf Hitler to understand the wonder of his statesmanlike show, which is already based in these origins. Because it is not time which has changed the Fuhrer, but the Fuhrer who has changed the times. What still seemed like a paradox at the time has today long since become self-evident. And it became self evident not of itself, but due to the clear and uncompromising decision of a man and the tough and relentless struggle, until it had become established.

It would have been a cheap trick at the time to make social claims which could be all the wilder the further the Fuhrer and his movement became removed from the realization of the promises. It can also be admitted that for the first few years it would perhaps have been easier to recruit followers in this way. The Fuhrer refused to do this. He created for his move—ment a philosophical platform which, to a certain extent, became the major basis of his party and his government. The essential characteristic of this philosophy was the combination of the national and socialist principal which, in an extremely simple and easily intelligible way, joined together on a higher plane the actual driving forces of the time which were locked in a bitter feud. The fact that nothing needed to be changed as far as the programme and the philosophy, the flag and the name of the National Socialist movement were concerned when it came to power shows clearly how farseeing and statesmanlike the foundations of the National Socialist rise were laid from the very beginnings of the Party. The Fuhrer had seen to it that no compro—mises were made. It combined the greatest irreconcilability as far as principles were concerned

After the New Year's Diplomatic
Reception in 1936.

The Fuhrer and the Reich's
Foreign Minister, von Neurath.

**Adolf Hitler meets Mussolini
in Venice in 1934.**

**In the Chancellery: The Fuhrer
and his Chief of Staff, Lutze.**

with the greatest flexibility as far as methods and actions were concerned. From the first day of its existence it lead a life and death struggle against parliamentarianism, until it destroyed it. It did not evade the terror of the Marxist parties with cautious and cowardly speeches, but pitched brute force against brute force. If its first bold attempt at arson in its conquest of power from the 8th to the 9th of November in 1923 failed, later historians will have to investigate not only what was achieved by this, but also what was hindered by this. And we can already say today that their judgement will completely justify the action the Fuhrer took. How do bourgeois politicians usually behave in times after unsuccessful coups? They either fled abroad or claimed that they had not taken part. Not so with the Fuhrer! He stood before his men, was the first among the accused, refused to step onto any golden bridge built by the court or the government, offered no excuses, confessed openly that he had wanted to overthrow the government, and that he would do it again whenever the opportunity presented itself. Thus he did what was obviously the most dangerous and devastating thing to do at the moment, and in doing so actually saved the movement and his work. His conduct of the great trial before the People's Court in Munich is a statesmanlike act on the greatest scale. It shows all the elements of political action at its best. Here boldness was matched with logic, frankness with courage, contempt for danger with bold action. It was a last gamble where everything was won because everything had been risked. The self-defence against the non-government of Versailles and Weimar was elevated here to a high, moral principle and carried along in a wave of enthusiastic admiration hundreds of thou— sands and millions who up till then had only dreamed about it or had longed for it. The Fuhrer cannot be held responsible for the path the party took during his imprisonment. The extent to

59

which he recognized the tasks of a statesman which awaited him and his followers after his release is shown by the fact that he did not become involved in any of the attempts at unification initiated by parliament and which, on the surface, seemed to be similar to his own. Instead, he set about founding anew the old movement along the principles that had been laid down at its inception. A tough struggle, full of sacrifices and privations, to renew the prestige of the party thus began. For years it seemed as if the undertaking was hopeless. At this time the N.S.D.A.P. was not even considered to be worthy of the hate of its opponents. While to all external appearances little seemed to change, the internal, organic development of the party gradually resulted in a reconstruction of the movement and of its individual organisations. If one were to judge a statesman according to his ability to assemble together men of intelligence, character and vitality, the Fuhrer need not fear this judgement. Rarely has any period of history seen such an abundance of real experts as ours. It is easy to determine today that these exist. It was more difficult, however, to choose them from the vast mass of his followers, to recognize their talents instinctively and to allocate to them the position which corresponded to their abilities in the struggle of the Movement and later in the government itself.

While there were still only 12 representatives of the national socialist movement in the parliament in 1928, this figure increased almost tenfold in the next two years. The party once again stood before the public at large and was thus faced with a decisive test. It could, as every other party up to now, let itself be fobbed off with a few minor ministerial posts and take part in the regime; but it could also somehow continue the struggle it had begun and carry it through to the end under the motto: "Everything or nothing!"

The Chancellor of the Reich at the New Year's Reception with the French Diplomat, Francois-Poncet.

New Year's Reception, 1935. The Fuhrer speaks with the Doyen of the Diplomatic Corps.

Again the statesmanlike instinct of the Fuhrer led to the right decision. The struggle went on and found its particular trump during the German Army Trial in the Leipzig Central Court in the proclamation of the legality standpoint by the Fuhrer himself. Probably no-one in the regime had suspected at the beginning of this trial what a democratic paper in Berlin reluctantly stated at its end, namely that the actual winner was Adolf Hitler, and that the highest German Court had moreover given him the opportunity to confirm his legality principle by an oath before the court and the face of the whole world. This had never before been granted him because of his previous record, but now he could always refer to it in the continuation of his struggle against the Republic. This was the deciding factor, and the very thing which distinguished the Fuhrer from his adversaries. With this statesmanlike insight he had recognized the possibilities of the trial at its outset, and not, like his opponents, at its conclusion. He was obviously aware that he would have to carry through the principle of legality with the extremists of his own party, but he also knew that this was absolutely necessary if the party were to win unanimously.

The gradual breaking up and systematic dissolution of the bourgeois parties were the next goal. Two years later after untiring efforts he succeeded in toppling the Bruning Cabinet. The apparent tolerance to the government of Papen went until the 13th August, 1932, and here again the supreme moment for the real statesman had come. For the final time it became a question of settling for half measures or wanting everything. Any ordinary politician would have chosen the first option. Dozens of examples from Germany's past have shown this. As a true statesman the Fuhrer chose the latter. he was rewarded for this great and daring decision in the November elections in 1932 with two million votes. Then, in a never before seen con—

The Fuhrer and the Polish
Foreign Minister, Colonel Beck.

The Reich's Press Secretary,
Dr. Dietrich, shows the Fuhrer
Press Reports.

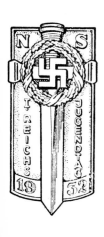

**The Cabinet of the Reich during the Proclamation
of the Defence Bill.**

centration of all his strength, he made one last onslaught against the regime in the Lippe elections in the beginning of January in 1933, and two weeks later he assumed power.

The alliance between Hindenburg and Hitler was the first symbol of the reconstruction. Here tradition and revolution shook hands. The brilliant statesmanship of the Fuhrer brought about a miracle in achieving a revolution of the greatest dimensions without major bloodshed by a reconciliation with the genuine traditional powers. Here is proof of a man of vision and instinct acting supremely to bring an innate law to its natural conclusion. Here, under the contempt of seemingly radical empty phrases, a grandiose change was effected, a world was turned upside down and a new world was created.

The miracle of German unification was the result. Having brought the traditional forces over to the government on the 21st of March 1933, Hitler then brought the German workers into the government on the 1st May, 1933. The occupation of the trade union headquarters at the strategic and only possible moment was an almost inevitable consequence of this process of remoulding the nation, and setting up of a four year plan to solve the urgent matters in German life was farsighted and extensive project which allowed time to attend to matters calmly and without tension. If, in the time which followed, the Fuhrer selected a very small but pressing number of matters facing the government, and by deploying any means at his disposal set about finding a solution for them, his actions in doing this were those of a statesman without par. Never was a revolutionary on a grand scale as far removed from any trace of hysteria and haste as he was. Never has a history-making politician worked as clearly and purposefully, and without great ado, as he did. And where in history has such a miracle been achieved under foreign pressure as here!

Boldness and daring went hand in hand in the Fuhrer's decision to withdraw Germany from the League of Nations. What filled the doubting with a sense of hopelessness was done here with a supreme assurance because it was necessary and had to be risked. It was the act of a statesman to put this monumental decision in his first year to the vote of the people them—selves. It was the act of a statesman to proclaim Germany's military freedom at the decisive hour and to announce it to the world as an established fact in the conviction that the time was ripe and that action was therefore necessary. Here we see his real mission. Here we see a man acting under a higher law. Here we see a man with an inspiration which does not come from the intellect, but from the blood.

In the Chancellery of the Reich.

English Front-Line soldiers with the Fuhrer.

National Day of Mourning, 1934. The Celebration
in the Berlin State Opera.

A restful pause between assemblies.

Federal President and Federal Chancellor on 1st May, 1933.

The Fuhrer in front of the Imperial Palace in Goslar
on the occasion of the Harvest Festival in 1934.

The Foreign Military Attaches at the Party Conference
in Nuremberg.

A German nation which is once again in a position of protecting itself by its own means, which has established the continued existence of its navy in an honest agreement with England, which today once again takes its place as a great power amongst other nations, which in increas— ing measure has aroused the admiration, or at least the envy, of the whole world, which is emer— ging more and more clearly as the most important element in world peace — these are the results of a statesmanlike development which led from the seven man party in Munich to the great power that is the German Reich today. A host of decisions is involved in this development. Altogether they give a picture of a fantastic and meteoric rise which will undoubtedly be praised as the greatest political miracle of the twentieth century by later historians. Here we see the results of an infallible feeling for what is possible and what is impossible at the time. Here clarity of direction was combined with purposeful action. Here we see the workings of an incredibly pure political instinct which achieved miracles because it believed in miracles.

Today Germany houses a different nation from the one it housed ten years ago. It owes its strength and its belief to the sure and unwavering leadership of a true statesman who not only knows what he wants, but also wants what he knows. He belongs to the few chosen men of history, because he is great enough to be an ordinary man, and ordinary enough to be great.

A sitting of the Reich Governors in the Chancellery
under the Chairmanship of the Fuhrer.

The Fuhrer welcomes a Japanese Navy Delegation in 1934.

Labour Day, 1934. Youth rally in the Berlin Lustgaiten on
the 1st of May. The Fuhrer departs after his great
speech to the youth.

A child presents the
Fuhrer with a gift.

The Fuhrer.

The bloodflag of 9th
November, 1923.

On the Tempelhof Field on the 1st of May.

The Fuhrer and the German Worker
by Dr Robert Ley *

The change which has taken place in the German nation since it has been conquered by national socialism can be seen most clearly in the attitude which the worker has assumed towards the new German government, and in the esteem which the worker and his work have found in the government.

*The N.S. Chief of Party Organization

The Fuhrer lays the foundation wall of the community
hall in the Adolf-Hitler-Koog.

**Young workers with the Fuhrer in the Chancellery on the
1st of May, 1934.**

Workers as a social class came into being at a time when liberalistic thoughts became the prevalent ideology in Europe. Liberalism has always viewed work as something unpleasant, almost dishonourable. Its highest ideal was to live off the work of others. Man's most desir— able goal no longer lay in helping to build the future of the nation, contributing his labours and deriving joy in doing so, but in discarding as quickly as possible the unpleasant situation of having to work and then living as a pensioner or from his interest, ideally also drawing more money from the management of his wealth and properties, or as a middleman in trade. It is obvious that such an attitude to life necessarily led to a down-grading of the work ethic, and we can reproduce the scale of worth of any work and its standing in the following way: At the top of the ladder there is the unemployment of the well-to-do, then work involving monetary or goods trade, then intellectual work and finally manual work.

This was really the dirtiest and most debasing thing which could happen to an individual, and whoever was unfortunate enough to have to work with his own hands to earn his living, was already fully degraded and excluded from the "better" circles of society. He was "imposs— ible". Just how deeply this liberalistic attitude poisoned popular sentiment is shown by the mere fact that even the worker himself, who day after day had to slave away at his job, saw himself almost as an outcast and scraped together all his pennies to enable his son to become "something better", perhaps a craftsman. The son in turn used every penny of his meagre earnings to send his son to a grammar school, or at least to some better school, however hard the son found Latin and Mathematics. The father himself did not specifically say that he did this so that his son may one day have an easier life, or be better equipped for life, in short, that he may have things better than the father, but so that one day in the future he may be something better than the future.

Can the insanity of this way of thinking be understood? This was the sort of insanity which was systematically supported by Marxism, which took great pains to reinforce further the infer— iority complex of the German working man imposed on him from above by liberalistic arrogance. Marxism continually dinned into the worker the feeling that he was a "disinherited person", a mere "proletarian", and that his hatred should therefore be directed at the "better" class.

What an execrable crime committed in the name of Liberalism and Marxism, caste spirit and class spirit, and class hatred!

Under Marxist enticement the worker thought he was improving his working conditions by refusing to work, under Liberal stultification large numbers of "educated" people preferred to go hungry rather than dirty their hands with solid work. The German saying "Arbeit schandet nicht"* was corrupted to "Arbeit schandet!"** The propertied and well to do saw in the

*"Work is not degrading"
**"Work is degrading!"

71

worker a lowly slave. The worker took his revenge by viewing employers as leeches and para—sites, and treating them as such in his dealings with them. However, neither group noticed that their attitude and consequent dealings would soon destroy the nation to which they both belonged for better or for worse.

This is where the incredible work of Adolf Hitler begins. He recognized that it was not a question of either the haves or the have nots, the employer or the employed, and that Marxism was not to be wiped out without the eradication of an arrogant and reactionary Liberalism, and he instilled a completely new and at the same time age old set of values into the nation. His short, lucid sentences made the nation sit up and listen. At first only a few, then more and more, and finally everyone came to see that for a whole century they had been wandering about in deepest terrible darkness. It was as if a blindfold had been taken from their eyes and suddenly they were bestowed with a new insight. In the light of this new insight everything which up to now had been hostile, and had seemed to be an irreconcilable difference, became deadly enemies to this insubstantial void. However, the Fuhrer taught one thing: You are nothing, your nation is everything. When you work, you work for the nation. Work is therefore an honour. There is no distinction in work. The work of a general director has no more intrinsic worth and is no better than the work of a street cleaner. It does not depend on what sort of work you do, but how you do your work. Anyone who does not work loses his honour in the national community. Work is not degrading, but enobling, irrespective of whether it is achieved with the mind or the sweat of your brow. Disgrace is brought about only by leading a parasitic existence and showing contempt for a working national comrade.

German workers love their Fuhrer.

With the workers in Siemensstadt.

Driving through a throng of well-wishers.

At the Blohm and Voss Shipyards in 1934.

And these sentences did not remain mere theory. If perhaps in 1933 the German worker, mislead by Marxism, and the reactionary stultified Liberals were sceptical and believed that national socialism may not have been totally serious with this philosophy of life, this attitude changed in no time. Today the German worker is the proudest follower of the Fuhrer who rescued him from his proletarian existence, restored to him and his work the honour of which Liberalism and Marxism together had robbed him, who finally gave back to him what he had always been struggling for deep in his soul, namely to be a respected man amongst his fellow men, to be worth just as much in his work as the next man, distinguished only by his achieve—ment and his efficiency.

When this came about, the German workers followed the Fuhrer with great enthusiasm, each one of them unanimously stood behind the leading worker of the Reich, and even the liberals among the propertied class changed their ideas to the national socialist way of thinking. In the third year of the national socialist Reich this new work ethic found its outward expression in the final stabilisation of the German Labour Front as an organisation which includes all creative German men, from the general director to the apprentice. From this day on there are in Germany only German working men and German businesses. The nobility of Work reigns supreme in Germany.

However, this could only be achieved because every single person in the German nation learnt a new way of thinking and began to look at the world from the point of view of national socialism. The Fuhrer once said: "Whoever wants to be a true socialist must personally have suffered need." The German working masses know that the Fuhrer himself was for many years a manual worker and personally experienced the pains which are associated with labour—ing from morning until evening, in sun, rain and wind, in frost and heat. Only such a man could

think the thought behind national socialism. He knew what he was talking about when he spoke of the honour of work, and the masses understood it exactly. Here is the mysterious bond which links the German worker with his Fuhrer. He freed the worker from his slave-like existence and gave him back the honour of the free man. Thus national socialism today rests safely and soundly on the work force. Thus it is therefore only a matter of course that on the national holiday of the German nation on the 1st of May the Fuhrer should welcome in the Chancellery delegations of German workers, and in these delegations is represented the whole of the German workforce, white collar workers and blue collar workers. They come as guests of the nation from all the gaus of the Reich, by aeroplane and by train, and they stay in the great hotels of the metropolis. They bring the Fuhrer the gifts of German industry, the greetings of their comrades and the assurance of their loyalty, their love and their faith. They all come face to face with him before they drive with him to the massive rallies on the day of German work.

If, individually, there are still many things to be improved, if mistakes still occur here and there, and difficulties arise due to need and lack of judgement, if disappointments are still with us, if the material situation of the work force has not yet improved, if in some areas there is still evidence of self—interest and meanness, if there are still some people unwilling to accept the new gospel of the honour of work — these are all only minor, peripheral things. The worker is not concerned by this, because the word stands and the word must be left standing, the word of the nobility of work. Only from such a way of thinking can the activity of the German Labour Front be understood. Before, who would have concerned himself with the state of working conditions in which the German worker laboured for his nation? Today the Department of "Beauty of Work" has the responsibility of ensuring that the German working man carries

Reichsparteitag, 1935. The Fuhrer with Dr. Ley
inspecting a troop of workers.

74

on his work in dignified places and not in ramshackle sheds. Through "Strength through Joy" the German worker has time for holidays and relaxation, today he wanders happily and often for the first time through his beautiful fatherland, today he travels in his own ships to the magic of Southern Seas and lands, to the exalted beauty of the North.

Today, like every German national comrade, the worker enjoys the magnificent achieve—ments of German drama and German music, the best German orchestras, the best German opera and theatre performances and the best German films. He is entertained by programmes on the radio. He can take up every sort of sport. However, the content of his new existence is not characterised by hedonism, diversion and physical impulses, but by the noble and genuine pleas—ure he derives from his physical labours, from nature and culture. Whoever works hard should also be able to enjoy himself thoroughly, so that his value to the nation increases. No longer does the scourge of unemployment cripple the nation. Millions have already returned to their place of work, and those still waiting are under the care of the whole nation. Trustees ensure that the worker's rights and his honour are not affected, and the manager is just as responsible for the well-being of his employees and his employers, working with him, are responsible for the prospering of the business in which they work together. Here the fundamental difference bet—ween national socialism and the past is most clearly marked: everywhere in the past there were only presidents and chairmen, and then the common herd. There were chairmen of the boards, of the administration, of the parties, of the unions and employers groups, of social benefits committees and strike committees. Today we have the Fuhrer of the whole nation, and behind him the Fuhrer (or leaders), of whom each one has his particular field or a group

The Fuhrer at the Automobile Exhibition of 1935 in Berlin.

Laying of the Foundation Stone for the new new Reich's Bank, May 1934.

of people. Before, everyone chaired a meeting of others, everyone took to their chairs, and there was no goal or defined path. Today there is direction, a defined path and a goal; everyone has been broken up and everyone marches behind the Fuhrer.

In language and in speech the whole difference between the two times is also expressed.

Everyone, however, knows that he has only one man to thank for all this, and that man is Adolf Hitler, who created national socialism, put the common good before self-interest, put an end to class struggle from above and below, from the left and the right, by proclaiming the honour of work and of service to the nation. So that this doctrine, which has made the German worker the upholder of the government, may never again go astray, the National Socialist Labour Service has been created. Here every German national comrade, before he is allowed to work for personal gain, must contribute with his own hands to the benefit of the nation.

The Fuhrer dispelled from Germany arrogance and contempt, jealousy and hatred where work and possessions were concerned. He gave to his people pride and honour in being a worker, and the responsibility of serving the whole nation. The German worker today is happy to be a free man in a free country. He is the leading worker in the world. Centuries to come will envy him this position. He, however, thanks from the bottom of his heart the man who gave him all this — the Fuhrer.

A visit to the Bavarian Motor Works.

A rest on a country road.

The Mercedes Benz Racing Car built at the
Instigation of the Fuhrer.

Visit to Eastern Prusssia.

A statesman among the workers carries himself like this.

Greeting the troops.

77

A visit to the industries of Rhineland-Westphalia.

A visit to a Factory. A Representative of the workforce greets the Fuhrer.

The Labour Service attends to land reclamation.

International Automobile Exhibition in Berlin, 1935:
The Protector of the Automobile Industry.

This is how the German farmers greet their Fuhrer
Adolf Hitler. Buckeberg, 1935.

Federal Chancellor Adolf.

The Fuhrer and support
staff.

The Fuhrer and his
favourite dog.

The Fuhrer and the Arts
by Dr Joseph Goebbels

Art is the most noble activity of the human soul and the human imagination. It is the con—cretization of feeling. What the artist harbours in his heart he expresses through art. Heightened feelings require heightened forms of expression. The artist is able to parade his inner spirit. He puts words to what the masses at large sometimes experience only as a vague and dulled longing, or he expresses it through his music, in stone or in marble. At all times art has elevated and shaken mankind. It has transported men out of the dreariness of their mundane existence into a better world. Indeed, whole eras of a new cultural and historical development have been trans—figured and immortalized through art.

This is also why artists, as divinely gifted beings who give meaning to the innermost secrets of human life, have always stood next to great men in all other fields. "The singer accompanied the king" has always been the most distinguished commandment of the really great, flourishing eras of human culture and history.

This does not mean that rising historical eras need necessarily also include great artistic events. On the contrary: usually they tend to follow each other. Either a flourishing of the arts and sciences leads to great historical change, or great historical change leads to a flourishing of the arts and sciences. This may well be due to the fact that either one or the other draws the outstanding, dynamic men so that these are either taken and used in the service of politics or in the service of art. As a result any other potentials which these men have may remain dormant and are never exploited.

In the Berlin Philharmonic Hall. The Fuhrer at a concert of
the Philharmonic Orchestra conducted by the Director of
Music, Wilhelm Furtwangler.

81

On the occasion of the transference of a valuable manuscript acquired by him, the Fuhrer is shown the treasures of the Bavarian State Library.

However, it is not possible to generalize in this regard. There have been statesmen who were worlds removed from any artistic aspirations, who were so completely interested in and caught up in technical and scientific matters, that they scarcely had any time, inclination or desire left to concern themselves with purely intuitive values. They lacked the profound capacity for understanding the actual nature of art which is necessary to become captured by it and to serve it with devotion and passion.

There have also been many soldiers who were nothing more than soldiers, and who had no desire to be anything more. We are talking here about the outstanding organisers, instructors, educators and immortal corporals whose campaigns shook the world. Such statesmen and sold—iers brought about historical developments which were not directly the result of artistic endeav—ours, and therefore only indirectly touched on the realm of art.

Things are different with those statesmen and soldiers whose nature and whose work is based less on reason than on feeling, and who drew more on their imagination than on the rational consideration of their strengths. These are the true great men in the domain in histor—ical creation. They are therefore closest to the artistic nature because they are made of the same elements. To generations to follow their miraculous and inexplicable existence makes them appear to be the heralds and shapers of a destiny which ruled over them untuitively, and which will still be visible for centuries to come.

In our own history men like Frederick the First and Field Marshall von Moltke belong in this category of great historical figures. By nature and predisposition they were sensitive artistic natures who stood as God's apprentices at the spinning wheel of time. Their forceful presence put a stamp on a period of evolution. It is not intended to downgrade the activities of those other statesmen and soldiers who were purely technical in their approach and yet mastered their work to the last detail by their knowledge, diligence, energy and tenacity. Without Frederick Wilhelm I, the soldier and father of beaurocracy, as a precursor, A Frederick the Great would have been unthinkable. The former was necessary so that the latter could carry on his historical work. The former had to establish the government which the latter shaped. The former had to found and train the army which the latter mobilized and led to its historic victory in hard and daring campaigns.

In this connection, however, we must not overlook the fact that when both elements are not united in the one man, the original feeling for form is to be estimated more highly in its historical worth than the mere feeling for organisation, and that the feeling for form and its origins in an artistic drive and stems mostly from deep and mysterious intuition. The Frederick who wrote poetry and searched for wise, philosophical interrelationships, but who also sat in his dirty, threadbare uniform amongst his grenadiers at the bivouac fires at Leuthen, could hold his flute just as elegantly as he could wield his rapier bravely and determinedly.

The Prussian-German army has never been poor in such soldiers. The caricature of Prussian militarism which the world painted and held up to us could not have been further removed from the truth. Those soldiers who went through the school of the War Academy or of the Great General Staff were frequently not only military men but also philosophers of their craft. No—where has there been a clearer and more artistic stamp left on men than in these training instit—utions for the army.

German politics, however, has always been poor in such rousing and fascinating person-alities. It has had good craftsmen who knew their trade, but whose capabilities were also ex-hausted in the execution of it. Frederick the Great in his capacity as a soldier has a vast number of like-minded and similarly oriented men in our history. In his capacity as a statesman, on the other hand, he stands completely on his own.

This was the great and unique feature which placed the Fuhrer above those who have a purely aesthetic enjoyment of art. For him art was not an escape from life, but an escape before life. He turned to art whenever things became difficult and unbearable and he needed to draw force and strength from other areas in order to master life anew. Art is not weak and therefore does not train people to be weak. Its strong rules make people strong and keep them strong. Men who, possessed with a deep feeling for art, apply in the face of the nation great theories of politics and military strategy, are also acting as true artists, and for them politics and leading an army is therefore also an art. It is one form of art amongst the many others to which they feel deeply related and linked.

The Fuhrer in Bayreuth.

Visit to the artist's studios in Munich. Here with Prof. Wackerle and in the centre Prof. Troost.

A Visit to the Schiller House in Weimar in 1934.

The Fuhrer as a statesman belongs to these unusually rare figures in German-Prussian history. His most profound characteristics arise from his artistic nature. He is by trade a master builder, and later was often to say with a smile that in his youth he once had the intention of building, yet without knowing at the time that fate would call on him to build not houses but a government. His reconstitution of the Reich again shows in its original design the eternal laws of true architecture. His organisation of the government is determined by a logic which appears to be self-evident. It is carried out according to far-sighted and well thought-out planning with-out haste and tension, as under a master builder who knows Rome was not built in a day and that he has been called on to work not for a restricted time, but for decades and centuries to come. This is exactly what distinguishes the new foundation of the Reich by the Fuhrer from all prev-ious attempts. It rests on permanence and has an inherent architectural clarity, combining purposefulness and beauty in rare harmony.

The Fuhrer once, long before he came to power, said in one of his speeches: "If the German artists knew what I will do for them later, they would stand behind me to a man!" These words were lost in the wind at the time; without having to be reminded by impatient creditors the Fuhrer has been ttue to his word long before others dared to hope.

Just how strong his inner need for art is should have been known and suspected when, at times, before he came to power, faced with extremely difficult political negotiations or wear-ing tactical battles, he would sit of an evening alone or with a few companions unnoticed some-where in a box at the theatre. Here he would listen to the heroically intensified beats of a Wagnerian opera and hear in them the artistic harmony with his political nature. There are only a few people today who, to take an example, would have heard "The Master Singers" or "Tristan" as often as he has. He is a fanatical follower of art. He does not indulge in the middle-class smugness of professing to understand a genius after having seen or heard him once. He is still filled with a deep and almost humble respect for the talent and greatness which dwell in an artistic genius.

The drawings of the front-line soldier Hitler:
Ardoye in Flanders (summer 1917).

**The Drawings of the front-line soldier Hitler:
Shelter in Fournes.**

This respect sees and appreciates the man and his work as an entity. It is necessary to have seen the Fuhrer in the company of artists to understand the depth of his affinity with them. It is necessary to have had the opportunity of observing his untiring care for art and artists in his daily dealings to understand the meaning of both for him and his historic work. His respect for true artistic worth and work is to an extent a converted gratitude. What he means for the work of Richard Wagner in general and for Bayreuth in particular as a patron and directly involved friend and adviser is known only by those who have had the good fortune of being able to help him in his work.

To the little circle which usually surrounds him, those hours in which the Fuhrer, at a time when he had only just taken over the opposition lead, quickly sketched on loose bits of paper grandiose plans for the architectural redesigning of Berlin and Munich, will remain unforgettable. Here everything was in the right place and modern technology and thinking were combined with the latest architectural strength. Here, in prototype, there arose the face of these cities, cleansed and purified of the unsightly features which an era lacking in taste and style had imposed on them.

The monumental buildings of the Party, the new layout of the Konigsplatz, the House of German Art in Munich, the large-scale reorganisation of the Reichshauptstadt already reflected in interim projects - these are the first visible acts of completion of this seemingly incredible pre-planning at that time. It seems almost incomprehensible to an outsider that, not only did the inspiration and initiative for these monumental projects come from the Fuhrer, but that it is the Fuhrer himself who supervises and follows the execution of the plans in great detail and with expert precision. The Fuhrer always has time for a building plan. How often did we observe him in the studio of that architectural genius who unfortunately died all too soon, Professor Troost, and see his enthusiasm for plans and models which are now step by step becoming a reality. How often did we accompany him to new construction sites during their various dev—

velopmental stages and witness his great joy at the smallest detail which, purposefully and mean—ingfully, would form part of the whole in its completed form.

Even the pictures which he painted in his youth radiate this spirit. They are meticulously executed to the last brush stroke and reveal the precision and exactitude of the master builder. It is claimed that there are business-minded imitators who are unparalleled in their mastery of the forgery and copying of such small works of art, but they are unable to deceive the true expert. A genuine picture by the Fuhrer can be distinguished from a fake at first glance be—cause it has the imprint of the Fuhrer and contains in embryonic form all the artistic laws which appear in their full magnificence and monumental nature in his reconstruction of the state.

The man who, in his youth in Vienna, went without countless meals so that he could buy standing room tickets to the Viennese Opera to hear Wagner or Mozart, it today attached with the same artistic passion to a painting or a piece of sculpture. A stroke of luck gave him the opportunity of acquiring Bocklin's "Battle of the Centaurs". The Fuhrer has been seen sitting for a long time, motionless, filled with emotion and humiltiy, in the face of the greatness of true artistry as exemplified by this picturesque creation of a genius.

Who could doubt that these noble passions are the almost inevitable forms of expression of his artistic feelings which are also evident in his historical work? Are not, for example, his speeches a record of this three-dimensional and intuitive vision? Do they not, in their construct—ion, their clarity of style, in the monumental nature of their chain of thoughts, their precision but also variety of expression appear to be like a classical monument or like a Bach fugue? It is a poor view of a man to attempt to dissect his individual characteristics in an attempt to under—stand his personality as a whole. Here individual characteristics are united into a general picture, and its totality shows the contours of a man who feels and acts with the intuition of the artist, who in everything is and appears to be as he must be and must appear to be, and who, even if he wanted to, could not be or appear to be anything else.

The Fuhrer leaves an artist's studio in the Academy of Fine Arts in Munich.

Visitors to the Festival at Bayreuth greet the Fuhrer.

86

From its very beginning the Fuhrer imbued his movement with that burning impulse to modern activity which later gave it the strength for its great victories. He did not subordinate it to technology, but consciously placed technology at its service. For the Fuhrer has a positive attitude to technology. He uses the means and achievements of technology to the concentration of his will and his work. Even technology has its artistic side. Even a magnificently built bridge or a modern car constructed according to precise, almost classical lines, will always satisfy the sense of beauty in man. The autoroutes which the Fuhrer designed and which modern engineers built according to his plans are works of art of the 20th century. We can still see the Fuhrer on a sunny Sunday afternoon standing in front of the bold and splendid arch of the Mangfall bridge. In his face were reflected the pride and satisfaction of the man who can feel the eternal artistry even in the most modern technological testimonials to our vital time.

The Fuhrer is the sworn enemy of amateurism; he is of the proud opinion that it is more worthwhile to read, see or hear what is good and great ten times than to waste time with ten different average or below average works. If he is shown a film which represents an artistic success he will ask for it to be shown again a second time if the opportunity presents itself. Mediocre films are stopped after five or ten minutes.

Is it a wonder then that all genuine artists love and worship him from the bottom of their hearts? For he is their friend and, where required, their protector. He cannot imagine a life without art. No royal patron was ever as receptive to the arts as he. Where art is great and promising he will lend an encouraging hand, and nothing will be further from his mind than to treat an artist with condescension. And he, who had to fight his way to art as a penniless build—ing worker with severe material sacrifices, shows his generosity above all when it concerns bring—ing art to the people and the people to art. Ideas such as that of a national theatre have become a reality with his support. The great German cultural organisation, "Strength through Joy", finds in him its most warm hearted friend, adviser and patron. His sense of beauty does not have that unpleasant aesthetic trait that is associated with the selfish sybarite. It is at the same time a sense of what is purposeful and universal.

Not so long ago statesmen from various countries visited him in Berlin and for days on end discussed with him in the course of tough negotiations the questions of European reconstruction. They scarcely suspected that the same man who, morning, noon after afternoons defended the German right to existence and, in the manner of the economic or military specialist, had at his fingertips every figure and date to prove his point, would that same evening sit with them in his home and, deeply stirred and moved, listen to the quintet from the third act of the "Master—singers" or a song by Schubert, Schumann or Wolf. Perhaps they thought that this man had suddenly become someone quite different or that he had suddenly slipped on a new, unknown hat; and yet, in reality, he remained the same man, a statesman whose personal interests were almost unfathomable, a man who encompassed all the traits and possibilities of the German soul, an artist who moved amongst artists and therefore felt an affinity with them, because he also carried deep within him the artistic spark. Perhaps this hour gave to all those who were able to participate a deeper insight into the essential character of the Fuhrer than countless technical discussions and conferences. Here again there has appeared that fascinating strength of a genuine personality which enabled the great Prussian king to fight and come through his decisive battles not despite the fact, but because of the fact that he also wrote poetry, was an adherent of philosophy, constructed Sansouci, played the flute and, if the tough business of government and the military left him time, gathered around his table the most refined and illustrious minds in Europe. Because here, from what seems to be contradictions and contrasts, is formed the final synthesis of a great human nature and work which will survive for centuries to come. Here art has been transposed into military and statesman matters; the same strength is found here, it is merely exercised in different areas. In doing so it uses the same motor ener—gies which also stimulate and inspire art: imagination, instinct, inspiration, grace and motivation.

87

A Watercolour of the Front-line Soldier Hitler: The
Ruins of the Monastery in Messines (December 1914).

A Watercolour of the Front-line Soldier Hitler:
House with white fence.

Perhaps only a later time will be able to measure exactly what this means for Germany, for our people and for its national fate. We, on the other hand, have had the good fortune of seeing and experiencing the work and effect of a true genius all around us. Here the artistic feeling of a great man has not arisen from the need for luxury or frivolity. Here it is need in the true sense of the word and therefore indispensable from existence, life and work.

Perhaps the Fuhrer is best understood when seen in these terms. This is because for him art is that mysterious power which ignites the human heart "in all those grey hours, as life's wild dance crowds in on us" to new love. His attachment to art and artists, his solicitude and indefatigable care are only the payment and fullfilment of a debt and a duty which the poet has stated when he says: "Blessed art, I thank you!"

A Watercolour of the Fuhrer from the year 1914:
The Courtyard of the old Residence in Munich.

The Fuhrer leaves the construction site of the
Haus des Deutschen Kunst.

The Buildings of the Fuhrer
by Architect Albert Speer

It has often been the case in history that a head of government would to a great extent support the arts and, in particular, architecture. Thus a rococo prince of the 18th century would have castles and gardens built on which to feast his eyes, and give free rein to the architects of his time.

The Fuhrer also builds as a head of government; but he will never be able to build in this same tradition, as his great buildings, which are beginning to appear today in many places, are to be an essential expression of the Movement for thousands of years to come, and therefore a part of the Movement itself. The Fuhrer, however, created this Movement, came to power through its strength, and even today still determines to the smallest detail its final form. He can therefore not build as a head of state in previous centuries, nor as a benevolent client, even less as a patron of the arts — he must build as a national socialist. As such he determines, just as he determines the will and expression of the movement, the clarity and purity of the lines of the building, the severity of its appearance, the quality of its materials, and, most importantly, the new inner purpose and with it the inner content of his constructions.

Building is no mere pastime for the Fuhrer. It is a serious concern, destined to give expression in stone to the will of the National Socialist Movement.

It will be unique in the history of the German people that, at the decisive turning point, its Fuhrer began not only with the greatest philosophical and political reorganization of our history, but at the same time also set about the task of creating buildings with the superior knowledge of the master builder. These buildings were to bear witness to the political will as well as to the cultural greatness of our time for thousands of years to come.

After long centuries of confusion the will of one man has established a clarity and severity in building which, in its continued development, will have as its consequence a completely new style of architecture.

Just how closely the Fuhrer since his youth has felt attached to architecture, he wrote in 1924 in "Mein Kampf":

"As soon as my interest in social issues had been awakened, I began to study them with great thoroughness. It was a new and up to now unknown world which disclosed itself to me.

That I should zealously at the same time serve my love of architecture was a matter of course. Architecture seemed to me, next to music, the queen of the arts: my preoccupation with it could under such circumstances not be regarded as "work" but as the greatest joy. I would read and draw into the early hours of the morning without getting tired. Thus my belief that my beautiful dream would become reality, even if it took many long years, was strengthened. I was firmly convinced that I would one day make a name for myself as a master builder."

He himself tells how important these impressions from his years in Vienna were in the first chapter of "Mein Kampf":

"At this time I formed a philosophy of life and a conception of the world which became the rigid foundation for my actions. To that which I thought out for myself then I have only had to learn a few more additional things, but there was nothing I had to change.

To the contrary.

Today I strongly believe that in general all my creative thoughts had already manifested themselves in my youth, in so far as such thoughts exist at all."

This love of architecture which the Fuhrer developed in his youth has never since left him. However, through war and revolution, the foundations of state and national life in Germany were so shaken that Hitler, who even as a soldier began to become more and more preoccupied with political issues, decided to become a politician: He said: "Was it not ridiculous to want to build houses on such a foundation?" He was totally serious in his conviction that he should become a politician, and it was a difficult decision to say farewell to architecture, the art to which he always remained faithful, with which he always continued to occupy himself and which up to now has been his great love.

In the first turbulent years of his political struggle and during the early formation of the Movement he also gave the final artistically clear form to all its symbolic means of expression. He designed the swastika flag of the Movement — and with it the national flag of the German people; he determined the national eagle of the Party — and with it the national emblem of the German Reich; he was responsible for the ensigns of the SA and the SS; he developed a new structuring of his many rallies and thereby determined the basic idea according to which all the buildings on the Reichsparteitag site are erected.

The Konigsplatz in Munich after its redesigning by Adolf Hitler.

The columned hall of the Haus der Kunst Deutschen in Munich.

91

Design for the Congress Hall on the Reichsparteitag
site in Nuremberg.

Rostrum in the Luitpold Arena of the Reichsparteitag
site in Nuremberg.

In the course of many thorough discussions he designed and determined Nuremberg at
the party conferences not only the guidelines and programmes, but, in the course of lengthy
considerations, he also laid down exact arrangements for the setting up of the individual sub—
divisions of the Party, for the deployment of the flags and for the decoration of the various
rooms. In Nuremberg sketches and drawings by the Fuhrer from this time are still carefully
preserved.

At a time when all his energies are called on to achieve the great goal, his preoccupation with art is and remains not "work" but the "greatest joy".

At the right time fate led to his meeting with his architect, Paul Ludwig Troost, with whom he soon formed a friendship based on an affinity of minds. What Dietrich Eckart was to the Fuhrer as far as the exchange of ideas of a philosophical nature was concerned, Professor Troost soon became for him as far as architecture was concerned.

The first building to arise through the unique combination of these two men, and also the first small construction of the Movement, was the "Brown House" in the Brienner Strasse in Munich. It was only a renovation, but for that time, as the Fuhrer sometimes related later, a massive undertaking.

Here one can already see everything that was to be expressed even more distinctly in the buildings which were to be constructed after he came to power: severe and austere, but never monotonous. Simple and clear, and without false decoration. Ornamentation used sparingly, but in the right place, so that it could never be considered as superfluous. Material, form and lines combine to create an impression of nobility.

A picture of the Index Room in the Brown House, Munich.

The Fuhrer in Munich.

The Heiligendamm.

93

The Fuhrer and Rudolf Hess inspect the construction
of the Fuhrerhaus in Munich.

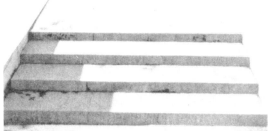

The "Eternal Guard" on the Konigsplatz
in Munich.

The Brown House in Munich.

The plans for this renovation were made in the same simple studio owned by Baumeister Troost in the back room of a house in the Theresien Strasse in Munich, where later the plans for the Konigsplatz in Munich, for the Huus der Kunst and for many of the Fuhrer's other buildings were to be made. These plans were to form the basis of a new style of architecture.

The Fuhrer has never received the plans for these important buildings in his official rooms. For years he has gone to Professor Troost's studio in his free time to engross himself totally on the spot and free from his political work in the plans of future constructions. The Fuhrer does not occupy himself solely with the major overall plans; he surveys every individual detail and every new assembly of materials, and much is improved by his stimulating suggestions. These hours of mutual planning are, as the Fuhrer has often confessed, hours of purest joy and great happiness. They are a form of relaxation of the most noble kind in the course of which again and again he finds renewed strength for other plans. Here he has the opportunity, in the few free hours which politics permit him, to dedicate himself to his love of architecture.

Many years before he came to power Hitler had discussed with Troost plans for buildings which only now are being executed. Already in the winter of 1931/32 he talked over with him the future formation of the Konigsplatz in Munich, and many splendid drafts have been the result of these meetings. And even before he came to power, as a result of these many discussions, the square already existed in its present shape in plans and models.

94

When the Glass Palace burnt down in Munich in 1932 and an inconsequential design for its reconstruction was put forward by the government of the time, the Fuhrer had one additional concern besides his many others, and that was that this imperfect plan would be started before he came to power. If one compares the model of this earlier design with the model of the now completed "Haus der Deutschen Kunst" built according to the design of Paul Ludwig Troost, then one can see more clearly than anywhere else from which other ideal world the Fuhrer draws his buildings.

In the irreplaceable artist Paul Ludwig Troost the Fuhrer had found his architect. Troost seized the Fuhrer's intentions, and always managed to give them the right architectural expression.

In his great speech at the cultural conference of the Reichsparteitag in 1935 the Fuhrer unveiled a memorial to Professor Troost with words that could not be more moving for an architect of our time. He said:

"We should be happy and proud that by some strange chance the greatest arch— itect Germany has ever known since Schinkel was able to erect in the new Reich and for the Movement his first and unfortunately only monumental works in stone, as memorials of the most noble and truly Germanic tectonics."

It is a pleasure for the Fuhrer to see the plans of a new building arise; it is just as great a pleasure for him to be able to experience personally the actual progress of these buildings.

Whenever he wanders through his building sites, often accompanied by only a few employ— ees, he is the complete expert. His numerous questions of a technical nature, either about the foundations, the strength of the walls or about problematic details of construction, are clearly put and usually unintentionally touch on some existing unsolved difficulty. Often it is in this area of engineering construction, when, after long consultations, all the experts are doubtful of a solution, that he comes up with a suggestion which usually proves to be logical and easily executed.

The Foyer of the German Opera House in Charlottenburg.

Our Beloved Fuhrer

The Fuhrer in a pensive
mood.

The Fuhrer in Postdam
1932.

The Fuhrer, Professor Gall and Architect Speer inspect
the building progress of the Haus der Deutschen Kunst.

A Meeting on the new Alpine Road.

Every new step in the construction and every new detail in the building receives his thor—ough attention and appreciation. However, all this pleasure in details never prevents him from seeing the imposing alignments which distinguish all his buildings.

The buildings of the Fuhrer are constructed according to technically proven principles from natural stone. Natural stone and Nordic clinker bricks are our most durable building materials. What may initially appear to be the most expensive proves to be the cheapest in the long run. In all technical considerations unlimited long-lastingness is always the prime and most decisive principle to follow. For the buildings of the Fuhrer are designed to stand as a testimonial to our great time for thousands of years. Once the immortal buildings of the Movement and of our government have arisen in all the towns in Germany, they will be buildings of which every individual will be able to be proud and of which he will know that they belong to the public at large and therefore also to him. It is not the warehouses and the administrative buildings of banks and big companies which are to give the towns their character, but the build—ings of the Fuhrer, created by him and designed by him.

About the appearance of our cities in the past and in the future the Fuhrer has written:
"In the 19th century our cities began to lose more and more the character of places
of culture and sink to mere mass housing settlements.
When Munich numbered only 60,000 inhabitants it looked as if it were to become
one of the first German centres of art; today almost every factory-laden suburb
has reached this figure, if not multiplied it several times, without being able to lay

the least claim to having anything of real value as its own. These suburbs and towns are mere collections of apartment blocks and tenement houses and nothing more. How any particular attachment to such a town is to be formed under such deplorable conditions is a puzzle. No-one will feel particularly attached to a town which has nothing more to offer than any other town, which lacks any sign of individuality and in which everything was done to avoid anything to do with art.

But this is not all. Even the great cities are becoming relatively poorer and poorer in real works of art as the size of their population increases.

What recent times have added to the cultural content of our cities is completely insufficient. All our cities live off the glory and the treasures of the past.

Our cities today have no monuments which dominate the cityscape and which could in any way be described as a symbol of the era. This, however, was the case in the cities of antiquity, where almost each one had a particular monument of which it could be proud. The particular features of an antique town were not found in its private buildings, but in its public monuments which were not destined for the moment but for eternity, because they were to reflect not the riches of a single owner, but the greatness and importance of all the citizens.

Even the Middle Ages in Germany upheld the same leading principle, even though its conception of art was quite different. What in antiquity was expressed in the Acropolis or the Pantheon, could now be glanced in the forms of the Gothic cath—edral.

The comparison between public and private building today has indeed become lamentable. If Berlin's fate were to become that of Rome, then all our descendants would have to admire as the most imposing works of our time would be the ware—houses of a certain number of Jews and the hotels of a number of companies, these buildings which express most characteristically the culture of today.

Thus our cities today lack the outstanding emblem of the national community, and one should therefore not be amazed if the national community sees no emblem of itself in its cities."

The great buildings of the Fuhrer on the Konigsplatz, the Haus der Deutschen Kunst in Munich and the party buildings in Nuremberg must be understood in this sense. They are a start, but therefore nonetheless fundamental, and it is the same with the residential buildings of the Fuhrer. We are standing at the beginning of a new development.

The fact that one always initially thinks of the great buildings when the Fuhrer's buildings are being discussed is no doubt consistent with the meaning the Fuhrer gives to the creations of architecture.

This, however, should not lead people to assume that the Fuhrer's work in the domain of architecture is exhausted with these buildings.

To the contrary.

From his own speeches we know the crucial worth he places on shaping the social condit—ions of all Germans in such a way that every individual can be proud of what the community as a whole has achieved. The great importance the questions of living conditions assumes in this matter has already been stressed by the Fuhrer in "Mein Kampf".

In his years in Vienna he became acquainted at first hand with the poor living conditions of the working class families. He writes:

"What I had suspected before, I then learnt to understand quickly and thorough—ly: the question of the nationalisation of a people is firstly the question of the creation of healthy social conditions as the basis for the education of the in—dividual."

Official statistics on completed dwellings (new or converted buildings) in the Reich show:

1932	159,121
1933	202,113
1934	319,439

These figures speak more loudly than words of the extent the creation of healthy housing has increased under the government of the Fuhrer. This increase will continue and will rise even more sharply once the great building projects which are necessary for our security have been completed. In the Fuhrer's own words, they are urgent, and therefore cannot be postponed.

Then the monumental buildings of national socialism will rise above the healthy houses and clean factories of our cities like the Gothic cathedrals above the gables of the houses of the town dwellers of the Middle Ages.

Here also the tasks at hand are immensely great, but the Fuhrer gave us all the courage required when he said in his speech in the cultural conference of the Reichsparteitag:

"People grow in stature in the execution of such higher tasks, and we do not have the right to doubt that, when the Almighty gives us courage to demand immortal things, he will give our nation the courage to achieve immortal things."

Adolf Hitler and his Roads
by Generalinspektor Dr Ing. Fritz Todt

Those who have come to know the Fuhrer as a statesman, as an orator, as the leader of the Movement and in his other capacities in the previous essays, will, on reading the title of this essay, be faced with the question: Does this statesman, this politician, the head of state of the German Reich in this eventful time, really have such a personal interest and the time required to become personally involved in such an abstract and technical concern as road con—struction? The following paragraphs have been written to portray the Fuhrer's attachment to his roads.

THE IDEA

As long ago as his time in the Landsberg fortress the Fuhrer spoke about the necessity and his intention one day to have roads built which would fully meet the technical requirements of the motor vehicle and which would connect the indiviual gaus of Germany with each other. In the 14 years of his political struggle the Fuhrer has used the motor vehicle almost exclusively in his travels and thereby has come to know the German country roads between the north and the south, the east and the west. People have never ceased to be amazed at how well the Fuhrer knows whole stretches of road, their features, their construction, suitable rest spots and other details. The Fuhrer values travelling overland by motor vehicle particularly because no other means of transport enables the traveller to experience such closeness with the people and the landscape. Someone once tried to calculate how many kilometres the Fuhrer had covered on German country roads in the 14 years of his political struggle. It would certainly have amounted to 500,000—700,000 kilometres, probably more. The distance covered by the Fuhrer on the German country roads in motor vehicles is therefore 12 — 15 times as long as the circumference of the earth. The idea of constructing a connected network of roads purely for motor vehicles arose on these trips and was completely formed by the time he took over power.

In summer, 1935, at the Mangfallbridge.

Twelve days after his appointment as Chancellor of the Reich, the Fuhrer attended the opening of the automobile exhibition on the 11th January, 1933. In his first official speech as Chancellor of the Reich he announced, besides other measures aimed at promoting motorisation, the commencement of a plan for the large scale construction of roads, and added:

"Just as the horse and cart once paved its way, and the railway built the necessary tracks, so must motor traffic receive the autoroutes it requires. If in the past attempts were often made to measure the standard of living of a nation in terms of the number of kilometres of railway track, in the future the number of kilo—metres of roads designed for motor traffic will become the indicator used."

Scarcely three months passed after that 11th February, days filled with the consolidation of the power he had assumed on the 30th January, to the 1st May, the first National Labour Day in the young National Socialist Reich. With this spring day in nature the sun also rose higher again for the German nation. The Fuhrer spoke about this, and about the departure of the divisiveness which had existed previously, the elimination of unemployment, the honour of work, the beginning of communal work which, orientated to one will, is the prerequisite and basis for the strengthening of a nation. Towards the end of this first speech about the Reich which was beginning to be built, the Fuhrer uttered these words:

"We are mounting a programme which we do not want to leave for posterity to conclude, the programme of the construction of our roads, a gigantic task which requires thousands of millions. We shall clear away all the obstacles against it and begin the task on a grand scale."

With these words the 1st May had also become a Day of Development for the road con—struction programme. From the idea of the Fuhrer the will became reality.

In the weeks which followed the Fuhrer received experts in road construction from Ger—many and from outside Germany, and was instructed by them. He then requested of the cabinet a law for the realization of his plans. The obstacles he had hinted at in his speech of the 1st May were surmounted in the course of a series of meetings. On the 28th June cabinet passed the law pertaining to the setting up of the undertaking called "Autobahns of the Reich". A few days later the Inspector General for the German Road System was appointed by the chancellor of the Reich at a short reception lasting scarcely three minutes.

INAUGURATION OF THE INSPECTOR GENERAL

Probably the hottest summer day of the year 1933 in Berlin was the day of the 5th July. After weeks of summer heat the buildings of the capital city had retained so much warmth that the short nights brought no relief. As on every other day the Chancellor of the Reich began to receive people at ten o'clock in the morning in the Reich's Chancellery. These receptions took place day after day with a short break at noon, and continued until late into the evening. Min—isters, Gauleiter, worker delegations, industrialists, expatriate Germans and many others alter—

The Opening of the first section of the Reichsautobahn Munich — Landesgrenze.

Work emblem at the beginning of the Autobahn Munich — Landesgrenze ("Let us begin" 21/3/1934).

One of the Fuhrer's autoroutes.

nated with each other to talk to the Fuhrer. Many indeed promised in the anteroom to limit their discussion to no more than ten minutes, but the Fuhrer himself would take up the subject matter, give his opinion, elaborate on the questions and involved himself in the last discussion late in the evening in just as lively a way as he involved himself in the first.

The Fuhrer had first asked to see the newly appointed Inspector General at one o'clock in the afternoon for his inauguration. However, as so often occured, the schedule was upset in the course of the morning by many discussions which ran over time. The appointment was changed to 7 p.m. with the explanation: "The Chancellor would like to see you last so that he has time for you."

When the Inspector General presented himself after the second last visitor shortly before 9 o'clock in the evening, the Chancellor said: "Come along, we're going into the garden. I strongly feel the need for some fresh air right now." During the walk which lasted one and a half hours in the garden of the Reich's Chancellery, the Fuhrer introduced his Inspector General to his ideas, spoke of coming developments in the traffic system, of the inadequacy of all those measures which were designed to meet only the immediate traffic needs, of far-sighted building and construction, warned the Inspector General of obstacles and difficulties, gave reasons for certain technical details, laid down exactly the minimum breadth of the roadway, the construct— ion of which was to meet the highest demands, determined the major lines for the main network and finally dismissed the Inspector General with the emphatic words: "I believe in the necessity of this measure and in the correctness of this beginning, and you must believe in it just as firmly as I do and act decisively accordingly."

The First Cut of the Spade
Frankfurt am Main
23rd September, 1933

In two and a half months of intensive work, plans and designs were drawn. For the beginning of this great undertaking, which was to stretch over the whole of Germany, only Frankfurt and Main came into question. Here a preliminary survey years ago had already looked into the possibility of a roadway purely for motor vehicles from Hamburg to Basel via Frankfurt. These preparations made for a rapid conclusion to the work on the blueprints. At the beginning of September the plans for the first section from Frankfurt to Darmstadt were finished. The first cut of the spade and with it the opening of the construction of this great undertaking were set down for the 21st of September. In the first meetings with the Inspector General Hitler had already determined that he himself would open the construction of this undertaking. For years the number of unemployed had risen in Frankfurt until there were approximately 80,000 in 1932. Now in the immediate vicinity of this city this great construction of the Fuhrer was to start. Thousands of workers were to be given lasting jobs which were to bring back confidence

101

and belief into the lives of the workers and their families. At seven o'clock in the morning the first 700 workers left the employment office. In the central square the Gauleiter and the Inspector General handed out the tools. From there the workers continued on towards the Main, their new place of work, singing and cheering.

The Fuhrer's plane landed at 10 o'clock. His trip through Frankfurt was fraught with great difficulties: The SA men who formed the barrier cheered the Fuhrer on and the inhabitants of Frankfurt, both old and young, again and again broke through the barrier, so that the trip from the airport to the construction site took more than an hour.

The place where the first spade was to sink into the ground was no festival ground but a construction site. In front of the embankment from which the Fuhrer spoke stood the workers and their families. The guests of honour were a little cramped for space. But here it was the workers who were the guests of honour. The Fuhrer said.

"We are today standing at the beginning of an immense task. Its significance not only for German transport and communications, but for the German economy in its broadest sense, will only be fully appreciated in the decades to come..............
In decades to come traffic will be dependent on these new great roads which we will build through the whole of Germany...
I know that this day of festivities will pass and that times will come when rain, frost and snow will make work trying and difficult for each one of you. But it is necessary, the work must be done. No-one will help us if we do not help our—selves."

The Fuhrer concluded his speech with the words.

"Go now to your work! The construction must begin today. Let the work com—mence! And before many more years have passed this immense work will testify to our willpower, our diligence, our abilities and our determination. German workers, to your work!"

To the cheers of the workers the Fuhrer seized his spade after these words, and stepped up to the construction platform. A train rolled forward pulling its large two cubic metre carriages filled high with earth. Slowly and thunderously the carriages tipped out the earth which was to build the six metre high wall at the embankment. With steady hands the Fuhrer dug his spade into the heavy pieces of earth. Again and again he dug his spade into the mound. This was no symbolic digging, this was real earth work! A number of workers realized that the Fuhrer would probably not stop until the two cubic metre mound had been properly levelled. They jumped forward with their shovels to help. The Fuhrer continued to shovel with them until the mound of earth had been spread in an orderly fashion and the first beads of perspiration fell from his forehead onto the earth. The Fuhrer laughed and stopped shovelling with his two unknown work colleagues when nothing more was left to shovel, and then walked through the work sites where the remaining 700 workers had begun their work in the meantime.

Flight around Germany.

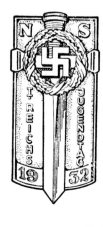

The Fuhrer's interest in road construction.
Inspection of the alpine road.

His roads lead Adolf Hitler to his people.

"Did you see how the Fuhrer even shovelled away the earth from the tracks at the end so that the carriages could move out again? Like a real labourer. He can really work, I scarcely managed to keep up", one of the two later related.

In the week after that first dig of the spade a supervisor approached the site manager of the Reichsautobahn. "Herr Oberbaurat, we must put a fence around the spot where the Fuhrer shovelled. Our workers remove handfuls of the earth after they have finished work and take it home in their bags. Even the women and the children take home souvenirs." Thus the Fuhrer's work and the attitude of the workers have ennobled work which up till then had fallen into disrepute as the dirtiest work of all. Many worker families today in Frankfurt treasure a small parcel of earth carefully than any valuable possession.

THE FUHRER'S PARTICIPATION IN THE WORK

The Fuhrer is regularly informed of the progress of the work by the Inspector General. In the course of these briefings the Fuhrer intervenes decisively in many details to influence the basic attitude of the co-workers to this work according to his will. In these discussions over the details it has happened again and again that a decision made by the Fuhrer has proved itself to be the only possible solution in the course of time. An example of this was the decision about the lines of the section on the southern bank of the Chiemsee in Upper Bavaria. Between this lake and the rising mountains there is a moor which is several kilometres wide. The crossing of this moor had caused severe difficulties for the railroad. The first design of the line for the Reichsautobahn avoided the moor in a wide arc to the side of the bank towards the south. The Fuhrer did not agree to this line which offered the road neither a view of the lake nor a view of the mountains. He requested that further and more thorough investigations should be made to determine whether a possibility could still be found to put the road closer to the lake. At his instigation further extensive drilling was carried out in the vicinity of the lake. To every—one's great surprise these further investigations revealed a rock-like ledge close to the lake. This ledge was just wide enough to enable the road to be built close to the side of the lake in accordance with the Fuhrer's wishes.

In the construction of the great bridgeheads the Fuhrer has also repeatedly made the final choice. One of the first great bridges to be tackled was the Mangfall Bridge near Munich with a length of approximately 300 metres and a height of approximately 60 metres above the base of the valley. From a contest which resulted in about 70 entrants the Fuhrer decided on the design to be used and thereby determined the type of major bridge which afterwards was to be built at various other places. The lines and shapes of the constructions which the Fuhrer himself determined are clear and simple, and at the same time ambitious and daring. Besides the shape his decision is greatly influenced by the question of the soundness of the construction. Cheap construction parts, such as hollow pillars and pylons, are rejected by the Fuhrer as they raise doubts about the unlimited durability. His constructions, like all his ideas, do not serve the moment, but the future: "What we build must still be standing long after we have gone." The decision of the Fuhrer can also from time to time be a rejection. The rejection is then pro—nounced and justified clearly. In one case the Fuhrer interrupted the continuing work on an unsuccessful construction and a telephone conversation with the Inspector General resulted in the immediate re-employment of all concerned.

For the German Alpine Road the Fuhrer also determined the bases of the routes himself and in repeated cases decided on different details.

MODEL CAMPS FOR WORKERS ON THE REICHSAUTOBAHN

The commencement of construction work in all parts of the Reich in the course of 1934 required workers to be housed partly in huts. These workers' camps were first constructed as they had been built for many years before in the building and construction trade. In summer these camps were just satisfactory. When winter approached it became urgent to remedy the existing situation, as these camps were inadequate for the workers of Adolf Hitlers's roads. A number of reminders to this effect to the industry were only partly satisfactory. In was diff—icult to remedy the unsatisfactory nature of this accommodation in a quick and satisfactory way after long years of workers having putting up with it. Finally the Inspector General brought the matter to the attention of the Fuhrer to seek instructions. When the Fuhrer learnt that the accommodation in the huts of the workers on his roads left much to be desired, he set changes in motion in the space of a few hours with his customary uncompromising energy which we have seen in similar instances. With the assistance of the Labour Service model camps were erected in the whole of Germany within a few weeks. The worker on the roads of Adolf Hitler is housed here in clean quarters. Meals are taken in larger rooms. Every camp has washing and shower facilities with hot and cold water and a communal room for relaxing after work. The Fuhrer himself drew the details for these camps in sketches. Through the Fuhrer's inter—vention in the autumn of 1934 the housing of the German worker has reached a standard which no other European country can boast of even approaching.

They see the Fuhrer for the first time.

Opening of the Reichsautobahn Frankfurt — Darmstadt in 1935. From l to r: Reich's Minister of War von Blomberg, the Fuhrer, Inspector General Dr. Todt, President of the Reich's bank Dr. Schacht, Director General of the Reich's railway Dr. Dorpmuller, Reichsminister Dr. Goebbels.

THE FUHRER AT CONSTRUCTION SITES
AND FINISHED ROADS

The inspection of a construction site or a stretch of road which has just been finished gives the Fuhrer immense joy. The Fuhrer shows an interest in all aspects of the work: the workers, the manner of construction, the housing of the workers and he also has a keen interest in the positioning of the road with respect to the landscape. The Fuhrer wants his roads to be bold and spacious, but at the same time in harmony with the landscape. The workers are usually very surprised when he suddenly walks out amongst them. Many have dropped their picks in surprise. Then, however, their eyes light up with the purest joy to know that the Fuhrer has come to their work. The feeling of happiness and joy which prevails at a construction site when the faces of hundreds of grown men express their delight in a way we have only ever seen in children in front of a Christmas tree is totally unimaginable. As a rule the workers stay at their spots and, after their initial surprise, continue to work. In doing so they show their capacity for work. The Fuhrer speaks with individuals, particularly with older workers. 60—70 year olds are no exceptions at these sites. To one 70 year old the Fuhrer said near Darmstadt: "When I am as old as you I would like to still be able to work as you are doing now."

The first trips over completed stretches of road inspire the Fuhrer. The traffic counts interest him, particularly as they confirm the interest of private and commercial motor travel in the new roads. The stretch from Heidelberg to Frankfurt am Main was christened by the Fuhrer with a picnic. He came for the first trip a few days before the section was opened to traffic on the way from Mittelbaden after the Rheinland. According to the Inspector General the Fuhrer determined that a rest stop should be made at a suitable picnic spot. In the magnificent autumnal beech forest the Fuhrer's cavalcade left the Autobahn and Kannenberg, the provisions master, produced a splendid repast in the woods. After such a trip over a section of road which has just been completed one later hears from those who had been present just how enthusiastically the Fuhrer speaks about his roads.

Thus the roads of Adolf Hitler come into being in close connection with their creator. The immense importance of these completed roads for the future development of transport and communications has been repeatedly emphasised by the Fuhrer himself: "In a few years these streets will be one of the most powerful means of promoting an increase in motor traffic, and with it in productivity, the extent of which is still inconceivable today, but also an annual attraction for many hundreds of thousands of foreigners, because after the completion of the Autobahns Germany will be able to lay claim to having by far the most modern network of auto-routes in the world" (15th February, 1935 at the opening of the Automobile Exhibition).

Far beyond the borders of Germany countries are observing the road construction of our Fuhrer. Almost weekly official and private groups of foreign guests come to visit the construction sites or the completed stretches of the Reichsautobahns. The enthusiasm and admiration with which they observe the Fuhrer's gigantic work are expressed in their letters and their newspapers. From the many foreign press agencies one has written:

"As the pyramids tell of the history of the pharaohs and the Roman roads testify to the power of the Roman emperors, so the magnificent autoroutes will serve to remind the German nation of the most outstanding figure in its history, a national comrade, once without name and position, who from nothing and without external help, created a new Reich merely through his own strength and imposed his will on the fate of the whole nation."

The Fuhrer travels on the Rhein to attend the transfer of
the Saar in 1934 on the Ehrenbreitstein.

The Federal President and the
Federal Chancellor.

Viewing the S.S. Troops.

Braunschweig March, 1931.

The Fuhrer and Troop
Leader Roehm.

106

In the city of the party conferences. At the window of
the hotel "Deutscher Hof" in Nuremberg.

OUR HITLER

Radio Address to the German Nation on the

Occasion of the Fuhrer's Birthday

by Dr Joseph Goebbels

However often the Fuhrer must show himself to thousands, at times hundreds of thousands, of people at mass gatherings, at receptions or at state functions as the representative of the Party and the German nation, and covnerse with them, just as often the Fuhrer consciously avoids all demonstrations and honours which are aimed only at him and him alone. It is this attitude which has led to his spending his birthdays in some little village or in a little town in Germany which previously had been generally unknown. Just how strongly the Fuhrer impresses his closest colleagues by his very humane and very personable nature can be felt in the radio speeches which Reichsminister Goebbels has given to the German nation on all radio stations on the occasion of the Fuhrer's birthdays. The text of the third speech on the 20th April, 1935, particularly merits being recorded within the covers of this work.

Ladies and gentlemen, my National Comrades! Two years ago already, on the 20th April, 1933, after Adolf Hitler had been in power for a mere three months, I gave an address to the German nation on the radio on the occasion of the Fuhrer's birthday. Just as then it is not my intention today to read out to you a glowing editorial. I leave that to better stylists. Nor shall I endeavour to honour the historical work of Adolf Hitler. On the contrary. Today, on the occasion of the Fuhrer's birthday, it is time, I think, to present to the whole nation Hitler, the man, with all the charm of his personality, the mysterious magic and the immense strength he radiates. There is probably no longer anyone on the face of this earth who does not know him as a statesman and as a superior national leader. Only a few, however, have had the privilege of being in his presence daily, seeing him at close hand and, I may add, consequently getting to understand and love him all the more. These few alone have understood the miracle of how and for what reason it is possible that a man, who a mere three years ago still had half the nation against him, today has been elevated above all doubt and above all ciriticism by the entire nation. If Germany now has found an unshakeable unity, then it is in the conviction that Adolf Hitler is the man of destiny who has been called upon to raise the nation up again out of its most terrible internal divisiveness and the humiliation imposed on it from without to the freedom its people have longed for.

The fact that one man through his work, which has at times necessitated hard and unpopular decisions, has captured the hearts of the whole nation is one of the deepest and most so wonder— ful secrets of our time. This cannot be explained merely by the force of his achievements, be— cause it is the very people who have sacrificed the most and those who must still make sacrifices in the cause of national reconstruction who were most moved by his broadcast and who are the most sincere and ardent in their love for him as the Fuhrer and as a man. This is the result of the immense charm of his personality and the magic of his pure and unspoilt humanity.

This humanity, as it is revealed most vividly to those closest to him, is to be the subject of this speech.

Like every genuine humanity, so this one is simple and clear in its being and in its action. This is revealed just as much in the smallest as in the greatest things. The simple clarity which is foremost in his political dealings, is also the ruling principle of his whole life. It is totally incon— ceivable to imagine him posing. His people would not recognize him again in a pose. His daily menu is the simplest and most modest that one can imagine. Its presentation does not change whether he is dining with a few close friends or with important state visitors. When recently at a reception for the gaus governors of the winter assistance scheme an elderly party member asked him to sign a menu as a souvenir after lunch, he hesitated for a moment and then laughed and said: "It really doesn't matter. Here the menus never change, and anyone may have a look at them."

Adolf Hitler is one of the few state leaders who, with the exception of a single distinguished war medal which he won as an ordinary soldier for his immense personal bravery, never wears medals and decorations. This shows his restraint, but also his pride. There is no-one on earth who could be more distinguished than he himself. Every sign of obtrusiveness he finds upleasant; but wherever he has to represent his government and his nation he does so with a composed and impressive dignity. And behind everything he is and does are the words which the great soldier Schlieffen wrote about his work: "More essence than appearance!" In him diligence and an un— tiring tenacity which reach out far beyond normal human strength combine in the pursuit of set goals. A few days ago when I landed again in Berlin at one o'clock in the morning he was still sitting fresh and engrossed in his work alone in his appartment. He had me report for close to two hours about the construction of the Reich's Autobahns, a topic which seemed totally re— moved from the weighty problems of foreign policy with which he had been dealing the whole day from early in the morning until late at night. Before the last Party Day in Nuremberg I was his guest for a week on the Obersalzberg. Every night until six or seven in the morning there was light to be seen at his window: the Fuhrer was dictating the great speeches which he gave a few days later at the congress of the Party Day. No law is accepted in cabinet which he has not thoroughly studied to the last detail. He is the most thorough and well-informed military expert; every piece of artillery and every machine-gun he has a specialist's knowledge of. Only those who are familiar with the finest details can inform him in such matters.

His work pattern is clear and precise. Nothing is more distasteful to him than nervous haste and hysteria. He knows better than anyone else that there are a hundred and one problems which need to be solved. Of these, however, he chooses two or three pressing ones which he has identified as the general problems and refuses to let himself be distracted by the gravity of the remaining ones as he attends to them. He knows that by solving the few very great problems, problems of lesser importance often tend to solve themselves as a result.

In attacking the problems themselves he shows on the one hand the firmness which is re— quired to carry through the principles, and the flexibility which seems to be necessary in impl—

Last Visit to Hindenburg before his Death in July, 1934.

ementing the methods. The Fuhrer is nothing less than a stickler for his principles and a worsh— iper of dogmas; however, principles and dogmas never come off badly because he approaches them with the superior adaptability of his methods and procedures. His goals have never changed. What he is doing today is what he wanted to do in 1919. However, in accordance with the situation at hand he has always been able to change the methods which he used in the past to achieve these goals. When he was offered the office of Vice Chancellor in 1932 he refused plainly and bluntly. He had the feeling that the time was not yet ripe and that the ground on which he was to be placed was too narrow for him to remain standing on. When on the 30th January 1933 a wider door was opened to him, he strode through courageously, even if it was not total responsibility which he was given. He knew that the foundation on which he was now standing was sufficient for him to begin the struggle for absolute power from there. Those who claimed to know better at the time understood neither one nor the other; today they need to offer their apologies humbly because he was superior to them not only in tactics but also in the strategic carrying out of principles whose champions they had set themselves up to be in arrogant shortsightedness.

Funeral Service for Field Marshal von Hindenburg in the
Courtyard of Honour of the Tannenberg Memorial.
The Fuhrer's Obituary.

Last summer two photos appeared in the press which show the Fuhrer's solitariness in a most startling way. The first shows him saluting a march past of the army from the window of the Chancellery the day following the 30th of June when he was forced to wash treason and mutiny away with bloodshed. His face was almost paralyzed by the incisive bitterness of the difficult hours he had just experienced. The second photo shows him leaving the house of the Reich's President after a last visit to the dying Field Marshall. His face is overshadowed by pain and sadness at the merciless death which was to rob him of his fatherly friend within the next few hours. It was with an almost prophetic foresight that on New Year's Eve 1934 he had already told a few of his close friends of the great dangers ahead for 1934 and that Hindenburg would be torn from our sides in the course of the year. Now the unavoidable had happened, and in the drawn features of one individual is expressed the pain of a whole nation.

This whole nation not only admires him but loves him with all their heart because its people feel that he belongs to them, is flesh of their flesh and spirit of their spirit. This is expressed even in the smallest and most trivial things of everyday life. There is, for example, in the Reich's Chancellory a respectful camraderie which ties the last SS man in the escort command irrevocably with the Fuhrer. On trips everyone sleeps in the same hotel and under the same conditions. Is it a wonder then that it is the most modest people in his entourage who are the most devoted to him?! They have the instinctive feeling that there is no pretence and that everything about the Fuhrer is natural and comes from deep within his soul.

A few weeks ago about 50 young girls, German nationals living outside the Reich who had spent a year in the Reich on courses and now had to return to their bleeding homelands, asked in the Chancellery if they could briefly see the Fuhrer. He invited them all to dine with him and listened for hours as they talked about their homes and their modest lives. As they were leaving they suddenly joined in the song "When everyone becomes unfaithful", and huge tears ran down

The Fuhrer on his 47th Birthday.

On the Morning of the 15th January, 1935. The Fuhrer thanks Gauleiter Burckel on the occasion of the Saar Victory.

their cheeks. In the midst of them stood the man who had become the embodiment of an eternal Germany for them, and who now sent them on their difficult way with warm and friendly words of consolation.

He came from among the people, and he has remained one of them. He, who spends two days in 15 hour conferences with the statesmen of the world ruler England, negotiating with polished dialogue and a masterly control of the arguements and figures over the fate of Europe, speaks in the same completely natural way to men of the people. By a friendly, informal "Du" he restores at once the self-confidence of a war comrade who approaches him with trepidation and has probably been deliberating for days as to how he should address him and what he should say to him. The smallest children walk up to him with a friendly and trusting nature because they sense that he is their friend and their protector. In fact, the whole people love him because they feel safe in his hands, like a child in the arms of its mother.

This man is fanatically possessed by his cause. He has sacrificed his happiness and his private life for it. There is nothing else for him than his work which fills him and which he serves as the most faithful worker in the Reich with deep humility.

An artist becomes a statesman, and in his historical construction his great artistry is revealed again. He requires no external honours; his most lasting and immortal honour is his work itself. We, who have had the fortune of being daily in his presence, shine only in his light and want only to be his obedient followers in the train led by his banners. Often enough he has said in that small circle which is comprised of his oldest combatants and his closest friends: "It will be terrible one day when the first amongst us dies and his empty place will no longer be able to be filled." May a kindly fate grant that his place remains filled for as long as possible, and that for many more decades to come the nation under his leadership will be able to continue along its path to new freedom, greatness and power. This is the most sincere and fervent wish which the whole of the German people lay at his feet today in gratitude. And like us, who stand gath—ered closely around him, so at this hour may the last man in the furtherst village join in saying:

"What he was is what he is, and
may he always remain what he is:
Our Hitler!"

Buckeberg 1934.

The Work Army. Reichsparteitag 1935.

Reich President von Hindenburg and
Reich Chancellor Hitler.

Hero Commemoration Day 1935. In front
of the Memorial in Berlin.

Adolf Hitler entertains prominent citizens of the free state of Bavaria.

Farmers with the Chancellor.

Reichsparteitag 1935: The Work Soldiers.

Germany's Present.

The Führer and the Wehrmacht
by Lieutenant Colonel Foertsch

Adolf Hitler was a soldier in the German army. He was so on a voluntary basis and with every fibre of his being in the greatest war which an army ever had to fight, in the hail of bullets of raging world battles, in dirt and mud and clouds of gas, in the very front line which for four long years bled to death for the homeland.

He was a keen observer. He understood what the November Revolt could not and was incapable of understanding if it were not to have its activity immediately revealed as outrageous treason: that a people cannot work if they are unable to protect the work place of even their smallest son from enemy attack, that it cannot cultivate the earth if the sword does not guarantee the plough. He also saw what the old army was lacking and how it had been sinned against in the liberal era of 1914 by the Reichstag.

Thus two basic facts revealed themselves to him: the restoration of German military freedom and at the same time the creation of a new German armed forces, strong enough to defend the German borders from any attack, and secondly, basing the formation of these armed forces on old idea of universal conscription and on the principle that military service is a service of honour to the nation. It is therefore not accorded to anyone unworthy or inimical to the people, nor should there be any preferential treatment or special considerations granted to any individuals.

With inner sympathy and great satisfaction the Führer saw that the Reichswehr succeeded, amidst the pacifism and defeatism, the treason and the dilapidation of the November Republic, in keeping the German Wehrmacht in form and even shaping from it a strong and useful weapon within the framework of the existing possibilities.

Day of the Wehrmacht, 1934, in Nuremberg: Air
Defence Gunners in position.

Rangefinders of the Anti-aircraft Battery on the Day
of the Wehrmacht at the Reichsparteitag 1935.

Coastal Protection: Marine Artillery defending the Coast.

Already in the early stages there began as a result a liaison between the Reichswehr and the Fuhrer of the NSDAP. Particularly the younger officers soon realized that here was a man who was the only one capable of rebuilding the German army once again.

A few days after the 30th January, 1933, the Fuhrer, who had just been made Chancellor assembled in the Ministry of the Reichswehr all the higher ranking commanders. In detail he revealed to them the essential features of National Socialist politics. He assigned to them their tasks and put them clearly into the picture concerning what he demanded of the Wehrmacht and what its duties would be in a National Socialist Germany. The public at large heard nothing of this discussion. It was only two years later that the new German Wehrmacht emerged to see the light of day.

When Adolf Hitler wrote his work "Mein Kampf" he remembered the old army in which he had served for four years as an ordinary soldier and then later as a lance corporal, and he remem—bered it with words which show today and always the great pride in the German Wehrmacht:

"The army was the most powerful school in the German nation, and it was not in vain that the hatred of all its enemies was directed expressly against this umbrella of national survival and freedom. No more splendid memorial can be dedicated to this single institution than the realization of the truth that it was slandered, hated, fought, but also feared, by anyone and anything inferior. What the German people owe the army may be briefly summarized in a single word: everything. The army taught absolute responsibility at a time when this quality had already become rare; furthermore it taught personal courage in an era when cowardice threatened to become a rampant illness, and the willingness to make sacrifices for the common good was already considered almost stupidity. The only people thought to be clever seemed to be those who knew best how to protect themselves alone and promote their own best interests. It was the school which still taught the individual German not to look for the well-being of the nation in the hypocritical phrases of its international alliances, but in the strength and unity of its own national tradit—ions. The army taught decisiveness, whereas in the rest of the community indec—isiveness and doubts began to determine the dealings between the people. In an era when smart-alecks were setting the tone everywhere there was a lot to be said for upholding the principle that a command was always better than none at all. In this one single principle there was still a robust, unspoilt healthiness which had long since become lost in the rest of our life if the army and its training had not ensured the continuing renewal of this elemental force. The army taught idealism and devotion to the Fatherland and to its greatness. It taught that there was a united people and not separate social classes, and here perhaps its one flaw showed, namely the institution of a yearly voluntary service. The highest achievement which can be attributed to the army of the old Reich, however, must be that at a time of general outvoting of heads it placed the heads above the majority. The army upheld the belief in personality against the Jewish-democratic notion of a blind worship of figures. Thus it also taught what the present required most urgently: men. In the

Announcement of the Freedom of the Armed Forces, 1935.

swamp of a general softness and lack of masculinity there shot out from among the ranks of the army every year 350,000 vigorous young men who in their two year training had lost the softness of youth and whose bodies had become as hard as steel. The young man, however, who during this time had practiced obedience, could now learn to command. The soldier who had done his military service could be recognized by his very step. This was the highest school of the German nation, and it was not in vain that upon it was concentrated the grim hatred of those who, out of jealousy and greed desired and wished for the impotence of the Reich and the defencelessness of its citizens. What many Germans were too blind to see or refused to see due do ill-will was recognized by the rest of the world: The German army was the most powerful weapon in the service of freedom in the German nation and the nourishment of its children.''

In one respect, however, the Fuhrer's opinion of the old army could not apply to the new Wehrmacht as it had to exist after the Treaty of Versailles. This was because it was not formed according to the will of the people. Its form was forced upon it from without. Barely two in a thousand in the population were allowed to undertake military service. Therefore the Wehr—macht no longer exercised the extensive, educative effect it once had.

Thus it was a matter of course for the Fuhrer to ensure that this professional army was once again replaced by a true people's army. Every soldier knew this as well, and therefore it cannot be surprising that the decision of von Hindenburg, the Reich President at the time, to entrust the Fuhrer with the office of Chancellor, was greeted with enthusiasm particularly by the Wehr—macht, because if any power in Germany at all could free the army and navy from the oppresive shackles of Versailles, then it was the power of this Chancellor behind whom marched the str—ongest political movement of people.

However, even in the ranks of the Reichwehr, it was clearly realized that this act of liber—ation could not be child's play and that the greatest difficulties would be encountered. But there was at the same time an unshakeable belief that the Fuhrer and only the Fuhrer would be in the position of bringing about this act.

When his decision of the 14th October, 1933, to turn his back on the League of Nations became known every soldier's heart leapt for joy because everyone understood that now the restoration of German military liberation had been achieved.

It is no coincidence that since that memorable Potsdam day the German army marched next to the SA and the formations of the party on all German holidays. This new army, which is a true people's army, and which knows no differences of background, wealth or social position, just as the party has never taken these into account, belongs to the people. It belongs in the midst of the people, and thus does not consider it a command but a matter of course that it should be amongst the people on these holidays, whether it be the 1st of May or the Harvest Festival, whether it be festive or mournful occasion, or whether it be the great Nuremberg Volkstag. Everywhere the Wehrmacht stands shoulder to shoulder with the national comrades.

Thus even in his great Reichstag Speech of the 30th January, on the anniversary of the National Socialist revolution, the Fuhrer could say about the relationship of the Wehrmacht to the party the following words:

"It is a unique historical occurrence that between the powers of the revolution and the leaders of a most highly disciplined Wehrmacht there should be such a warm and close association as there is between the National Socialist party and me as its Fuhrer on the one hand, and the officers and soldiers of the German Reichs Army and Navy on the other hand. The Wehrmacht and its leadership has stood in com—plete loyalty and allegiance to the new government.

The fact that the Wehrmacht has no special existence but is a National Socialist Wehrmacht goes without saying in a National Socialist government, but even in external matters this is expressed with pride and joy by the fact that every man who serves in it, from the Commander-in-Chief to the last recruit, wears the national emblem of the National Socialist movement on his uniform.''

The Launching of the Tank Ship "Admiral Graf Spee".

The Fuhrer amidst his Blue Boys.

A Visit to the Fleet.

119

The Fuhrer has repeatedly emphasised this and has described the Party and the Wehrmacht as the two pillars on which the construction of the National Socialist Third Reich is founded. With great clarity he explained that the Party was the political will bearer of the nation and the Wehrmacht the weapon bearer. Consciously and entirely of its own free will the Wehrmacht developed totally in the National Socialist sense in the new government and allied itself to the government for better or for worse. It is a straight line from the introduction of the comradely greeting with the divisions of the NSDAP, through the participation on all the festivities of the party and the government, to the introduction of the national emblem of the Movement into the Wehrmacht, its participation in the Party Days to the raising of the naval ensign decorated with the swastika. And the 'Duties of the German Soldier' have been written in the National Socialist spirit just as the oath of allegiance also expresses this: "I swear to God this holy oath, of absolute obedience to the Fuhrer of the German Reich and the German people, the Com—mander-in-Chief of the Wehrmacht. I also swear as a courageous soldier that I will be prepared at any time to risk my life for this oath."

The Reich's Minister of War, from the first day he assumed office, had left no doubts that the National Socialist philosophy would also have to be the irrevocable basis for the life of the German Wehramcht. During his addresses to the troops and on all other occasions he alluded to this again and again and stated that the vow of loyalty to the Fuhrer and his work was hon—ourable and sacrosanct. The Wehrmacht grew in the government of the German rebirth. The Reich's War Minister himself once put this into words in an essay in the Volkische Beobachter*: "It came as what it was, as the innerly organised, disciplined means of power in the hands of its leadership. It serves this government, which it supports from deep conviction, and it stands to this leadership which gave back to it the first and foremost right not only to be the bearer of its weapons but also to be the bearer of an unlimited trust on the part of the people and the gov—

The First Swearing in of Recruits of the People's Army at the
Feldherrnhalle in Munich on the 7th November, 1935.

The Reichsparteitag at Nuremberg, 1935: The Navy during the March Past on the Day of the Wehrmacht.

ernment. Today a military view of things penetrates the whole of the German people. The strength in which the Wehrmacht is carried streams as an elemental force from the source of a strong belief in Germany and its right to survival. Today the soldier stands consciously in the middle of the political life of a united people. Military service has once again become a service of honour to the German people. The Wehrmacht has stood up to the difficult test of discipline in Germany's darkest time, under incredible strain at times, and has won out. The action groups of the trenches of the World War which Hitler made as the foundation of the new national community became the starting point of the great tradition which the Wehrmacht inherited from the old army. It stands in close association with the whole of the people, proudly wearing the emblem of Germany's rebirth on its steel helmets and uniforms, in military discipline and loyalty behind the leadership of the government, the Fuhrer of the Reich, Adolf Hitler, who once came from our ranks and will always remain one of us."

* NS newspaper

Here one can read the very secret which binds the Fuhrer with the new army. It is the same secret which binds the Fuhrer and the worker, The Fuhrer and the farmer, the Fuhrer and the political fighter, because each one can say with conviction: He is one of us. The Fuhrer comes from the farm, he was a worker like millions and millions of his national comrades, and, as an ordinary soldier, he lay in the trenches during a four year war for the continued existence of Germany, again as millions and millions of Germans did. He was a soldier, a courageous soldier, who risked his life as a dispatch rider in the midst of the hell that was the barrages, and when today the old soldiers from the World War sit together with the Fuhrer then they talk about this time as they all risked their lives for the Fatherland and this now unites them in an immense friendship. They all know to whom they have sworn their personal oath, namely to the comrade from the Great War and in him to the legacy of all the fallen. This is what makes the Wehrmacht National Socialistic even from within: the Fuhrer is its Fuhrer. He will always remain the soldier who is prepared to ward off the enemy with his own life and who therefore also has the right to demand this of others. He is aware of the needs and worries a soldier has, he knows what he wants and what must be kept from him, and he knows this not from reports and hearsay, but from his own great experience. Thus it is obvious that for the Wehrmacht today there is no greater pride than to be associated with this man, and when the troops parade before him their eyes light up, their step becomes more determined and every muscle tenses to its greatest str—ength. The leaders, however, know that the new Wehrmacht owes its existence principally and solely to this man who in tough political negotiations and with rigorous attention to detail created the possibility of re-establishing German military sovreignty and restoring the old right of the free German man to military service.

However, the Fuhrer always impresses on the young soldier that this civil right to serve the people entails enormous responsibility and as much as the Wehrmacht will find in him every sup—port for what it requires, so he asks expressly that every soldier be aware that it is the sacrifices of the whole nation which allow him to carry out this civil right and bounden duty. Thus after the magnificent military spectacle on Party Day in 1935 in Nuremberg the Fuhrer spoke these fine words to his soldiers: "Whenever you have to make personal sacrifices in matters of obed—ience, fullfilment of duties, subordination, hardness, endurance and efficiency, do not forget, my soldiers, the whole of the German people also make great sacrifices for you. We make these sac—rifices in the conviction that no war is needed to reward us for them. You need conquer no glorious title for the German army — this it already possesses — you need only to keep it. Germ—any has not lost its military honour, and least of all in the last war. It is up to you to ensure that the trust of the nation will always be yours as it once was the army's whose helmet from its glorious past you now wear. Then the German people will love you, will believe in its army and make every sacrifice gladly and joyfully in the conviction that in doing so the peace of the nation will be maintained and the upbringing of the people guaranteed. This is the plea of the nation, its expectation of and request to you. And I know you will fulfil this request, the expectation and this plea because you are the new soldiers of the new German Reich."

Thus the Fuhrer and the Wehrmacht, the Wehrmacht and the people are one, just as the people and the Fuhrer are one, bound not only by oaths and promises, but through the common striving and the common will towards a free and united, strong National Socialist Reich.

Adolf Hitler's freedom speech to the world.

Berchtesgaden hunters.

Bombers over Nuremberg.

First Inspection of the Richthofen Squadron.

The Entry of the German Troops over the Rhein Bridge
at Mainz on the 7th March, 1936.

The new Tank Weapon.

The Fuhrer with the Reich Minister of War and the Commander-in-Chief of the Army in 1935 at the Manoeuvres on the Military Training Area of Munsterlager.

Our Luftwaffe.

On the Day of the Wehrmacht, 1935: The Fuhrer with his Commanders-in-Chief, from l to r: the Commanders-in-Chief of the Luftwaffe, Air Chief Marshal Goring, of the Wehrmacht, Field Marshal v. Blomberg, of the Army, General Freiherr v. Fritsch, of the Navy, Admiral Dr. Raeder.

The Nuremberg Reichsparte
glorious army on th

The "Lutzow" Tower and Battle Mast of the "Admiral Scheer" seen from the forecastle.

The Flags of the old Wehrmacht.

On board a Warship the Fuhrer visited the Norwegian Fjords.

The Greyhounds of the Baltic: A German Schnellboot.

A Visit to the Fleet in Kiel, 1934.

Tag der Wehrmacht Day in Nuremberg, 1935: Motorised
Heavy Artillery.

Once again we have tanks because of Hitler's action.

In August 1935, in Keil, the Fuhrer inspects the first German
Submarines.

The Fuhrer visits the Regular Service Ship, the "Schleswig-
Holstein" in the Port of Hamburg.

Party Conference on Freedom: The Youngest Drummers
in the Nation.

The Führer and the German Youth
by Baldur von Schirach[*]

The Fuhrer is paid hommage by our youth in all parts of the Reich, and to the concept of Adolf Hitler today belongs the picture of an inspired and devoted youth which cheers him on and serves him. We have become accustomed to it as to something totally natural. Whether on his journeys he drives through an uninterrupted guard of honour formed by this youth,or whether he is surrounded by it during the great festive occasions of the Movement, its marches and rallies, young people are always there where the Fuhrer is, always and everywhere declaring their sup— port for him. This picture to which we Germans have become so accustomed always appears to the foreigner as something marvellous; the mythical concurrence of the Fuhrer of the nation with the young generation belongs to those inexplicable things which the foreigner calls "the German miracle". There is, in fact, hardly a better expression for this occurence of complete unity, not only of all classes, ranks, and religions, but also of all the generations of our people. And this seems a miracle to us Germans ourselves: the fact that the Fuhrer succeeded in committing all age groups of our people to a common ideal, which each person tries to follow in his own way, i.e. with the strength over which he prevails. The younger ones and the very young follow it with that passion and power of enthusiasm which has always characterized a forwards striving German youth; the older people and the aged with the calm clarity of purpose, constancy and mature strength which characterizes their years. Thus Adolf Hitler raised an entire people to serve an idea. The ten year olds are the upholders of his work and heralds of his will with convictions

[*] Leader of the Hitler Youth

129

which are just as strong as those of the thiry to fourty year olds. Indeed it is particularly these youngsters who feel especially drawn to the figure of the Fuhrer because they sense with the unmistakeable certainty of their instinct that the Fuhrer has dedicated his thoughts and con—cerns to them above all. They know that he serves the future, which they themselves represent.

Germany has suffered greatly, particularly in its more recent past, from the conflict between the younger and the older generations. This conflict was felt in almost every family, particularly in the decade after the Great War. It is pointless to try to examine who should bear the blame here. Only this much will be said in this respect and that is that the blame for the obvious lack of respect and discipline which the youth at the time displayed did not rest solely on the youth it—self. These young people lacked completely any models in the older generation. The so-called "statesmen" of the time could arouse no enthusiasm in relation to their personality and their work, and were rejected or despised; thus all that remained to them were the unsatisfactory and false models provided by the film stars and sportsheroes. Should one reproach the young people of that time because they could not fulfil the expectations of their elders? Does not every educ—ator know that young people require great and above all heroic models in order to be able to take the direction which is necessary for the people? Men whose heroic participation in the World War should have been able to place the young people under an obligation were derided and abused by the press and even by influential figures in the government, and the heroic ideal could be mocked publically as an ideal of stupidity and go unpunished. In such circumstances it seems obvious that young people lost all sense of standards and manners. Because many mem—bers of the older generation behaved in a contemptible way, the young people concluded that all older people were contemptible. Because cowardice was praised, they believed in the cowardice

She says her little poem. The Fuhrer on one of his
election campaigns in 1932.

Again and again the Fuhrer is seen in pictures surrounded
by children. To the right is Baldur von Schirach.

of all men and completely lost their sense of right and wrong, reasonable limits and laws: The great sex trials against young people at that time, as well as the general crime rate of young people in the post war years, are still alive in our memories. They show us with horrifying clarity what can happen even to young people in Germany when they have no leadership.

Adolf Hitler has tried from the first day of his work to lead young people back again to himself. The fact that this attempt has succeeded to an extent that even the greatest optimists had never expected is due exclusively to his inexhaustible willpower and persistence. It is all too easy for the superficial observer of the years of struggle of the National Socialist Movement to overlook the painstaking attention to detail which, next to the great slogans and battles of the Movement, was required for its foundation and construction. Nor was the National Socialist Youth Movement merely handed to the Fuhrer; it did not arise, as many people seem to think, merely as a result of appeals in the press and speeches, but, as in all branches of the Movement, here also the Fuhrer strove unceasingly for years and years to formulate the guidelines of its construction until he announced the fundamental sentence according to which his youth leaders had to work. When Hitler had implanted the saying: "Youth must be led by youth" a new era in the history of the education of mankind had begun. Only a genius can simultaneously with one saying close off the past and open the future. With his slogan about youth education Adolf Hitler won all the young people of his nation to his cause. It is immaterial that at first this basic principle of the Fuhrer was barely understood; indeed that there were people who tried to mock it and make it sound contemptible as they did all programmatic utterances the Fuhrer made. It is just as irrelevant that the Youth Movement whose structure was determined by this rule com—prised only a few thousand. The only important and essential thing is that Adolf Hitler, from the spirit of the young people and with a capacity for understanding them such as no statesman or educator before him had possessed, set up and announced a programme which — we felt already at that time — was to build from the tiny community at the time the greatest Youth Movement in the world.

Apart from Adolf Hitler, all statesmen of the past and the present have seen the leadership of the youth exclusively from the older generation, in so far as they considered the leadership as a general task wich belinged to their generation. This had been handed down to them as a matter of course to which they gave no further thought. The older people relieved the younger people of responsibility and leadership within their own sphere of life. Large scale government youth organisations in other countries are conceived and run in this way; Adolf Hitler, contrary to all the methods of educating the youth up to now, has placed on the shoulders of the youth itself the responsibility for its actions. It was he who proclaimed responsibility as an educative force.

It belongs to the most moving testimonials to the inner worth of German youth that it did not dissappoint the Fuhrer's trust, but on the contrary, despite many aberrations, endeav—oured to justify a trust which it only ever regarded as an honour and a duty. Thus it proceeded according to the Fuhrer's guidelines and, working painstakingly and advancing step by step, has developed into a powerful community which has no comparison anywhere in the world. All this was accomplished without the compulsion of a law, without instruction by a minister, exclusiv—ely through the inner strength of the idea which propelled it. One should try to imagine the sig—nificance of the fact that even before the takeover of power by National Socialism the Fuhrer knew that the overwhelming majority of German Youth was behind him! The Reich's Youth Day in Potsdam took place three months before the Fuhrer's appointment as Chancellor, and is still the greatest youth march which the world has ever seen. The communist and social demo—crat youth organizations were already finished before the 30th January, 1933, and this was not because of brutal force, but due to the mental conquest of its members by the National Socialist philosophy. This distinguishes the Hitler Youth most strongly from the youth organisations of other countries: it was not allocated its tasks as an afterthought, but fought along in the decisive battle for power, made its sacrifices in this battle and in the spring of 1936 depended on a vol—untary allegiance which in the age groups of the ten to fourteen year olds alone comprised far over 90 percent of all young people.

Children's hands.

132

Young Germany greets the Fuhrer in the Election Campaign.

Hitler Youth as guests on the Obersalzberg.

Adolf Hitler even today follows up the work of his Youth Movement in all its facets. Year after year he receives in the Chancellery the boys and girls who have won the Reich training competition to offer his personal congratulations, and checks the buildings for youth groups by asking to be shown the models of youth hostels and their designs, and giving assistance in word and deed from his vast building experience. Often he makes contact with the young people themselves when in Berchtesgaden or in Berlin he invites home a group from the Jungvolk or the BDM whom he has met on the way. He entertains the surprised guests with coffee and cake, listens to the songs they sing and the tales they tell of their travels. The Fuhrer's birthday is perhaps the strongest expression of this close relationship between him and his youth. On this occasion there are on the long tables of the Chancellery thousands of little presents which boys and girls all over the Reich thought up to please their Fuhrer: handicrafts and original post cards, pieces of embroidery and travel books, all these things announce more eloquently than any words how much the thoughts of the young generation revolve around this man who has given our youth an existence in freedom and it is before these simple little gifts that the Fuhrer

**The 9th November in Munich. Hitler Youth in front of
the Brown House before their festive acceptance
into the party.**

pauses longer than before the more valuable, sophisticated ones. The presents of the Pimpfs seem to delight him the most on his birthday. In reality they have been made of the most valuable material: the love of the youth, of which Adolf Hitler is the recipient in a measure no-one before him has been.

The Hitler Youth is the only institution to bear the Fuhrer's name. This connection bet—ween the youth of our people and the leader of the Reich is the symbol for the deep and close relationship between Adolf Hitler and the youngest sector of our nation. Today every boy and every girl once again has the educative model to whom they feel committed and whom they try to emulate,and the indiviuals as well as the community have thus given themselves over to a common ideal. Reassured, the German people can glance into their future. The mistakes of the past have been overcome. The time of the generation problems is over. If once the youth groups of the political parties opposed each other in bitter feuds — today all young people stand united, and there where once the past saw the wealthy and the poor locked in bitter class struggle, the present sees the trusting alliance of young people whose socialist feeling of being alive is stronger than any feeling of selfishness. What some time ago seemed to be still impossible and even utopian to contemplate, has today become an overwhelming reality. Certainly these young people also had to make sacrifices in order to be able to fashion this reality. Many youth allian—ces of the past which honestly tried to reach a greater goal had to be abandoned to achieve the great community of all young people. And the Hitler Youth itself had to bury many a dead

comrade in order to be able to attain that final and complete unity without which no community on this earth can exist.   But the young fallen of this youth died in the belief in the Fuhrer and his future Reich, and the millions of young survivors are tied together in the same belief. They all feel themselves to be the upholders of the duty with which the Fuhrer has entrusted them, and they feel at one with him in their service to the greatness of the Reich. The work of Adolf Hitler can never perish because all young people in Germany have declared themselves prepared to serve this work dutifully and loyally for their lifetime, and then to hand it over to those who will come after them.

With such determination they greet the coming millenium.

Party Conference of Power, 1934. In the stadium with the youth.

After the Fuhrer gave her his autograph, she had the additional good fortune of being photographed with him.

The Fuhrer with the youth on the Reichsparteitag in 1935.

The Führer and the National Socialist Movement
by Phillipp Bouhler *

When the unkown World War soldier, temporarily blinded by mustard gas poisoning, dec—ided on the 8th November, 1918, in the Pasewalk Hospital, at a time when the pitiful stock market revolts had shattered the country, to become a politician in order to intervene personally in the destiny of his deceived and humiliated people, no-one could have suspected that a little more than 14 years later this same man would stand as Fuhrer and Reich's Chancellor at the head of the whole German nation. Only Adolf Hitler himself, knew the way. He also knew, however, that even in chaotic post-war Germany the political leadership would never fall on an individual who had neither reputation nor name, title nor wealth, and who could only bring to bear this knowledge and his personality and belief in himself. He knew that the path to power in the government — which offered the only possibility of a change in the wretched state Germany found itself — could only be stormed at the head of a movement carried by a winning philo—sophy and a fanaticism people believed in, and which in its nucleus had to be anchored along strict, organisatory lines. Who would Frederick the Great have been, without the instrument left behind by his kingly father, without the army by which and through which he gained his victor—ies? Adolf Hitler also created the instrument which was to provide the real basis for his politics. He created the NSDAP.

From the humblest beginnings, organically, he created his organisation. Based on the idea of the Fuhrer principle and a voluntary following, he broke first of all in his party with all parl—iamentary tradition and placed absolute responsibility at the top and unlimited authority at the bottom based on the democratic principle of the equality of all men and the rulership of the majority. While German parliamentarians haggled about the personal advantages of particular groups and exhausted themselves in fruitless voting as to what were the essential problems in the German nation, while under the eyes of the governments foreign hostile elements trampled on Germany's honour and reputation and squandered what remained of Germany's wealth, while the government stood by and watched helplessly as the German fatherland tumbled hope—lessly into the abyss of political and economic enslavement, Adolf Hitler was fashioning the instrument which was to free Germany internally and externally.

* Secretary General of the Reich Directorate

The Casualties of the Movement from the 9th November 1923
were transported to the two Temples of Honour on the
Konigs Platz. 9th November, 1935 in Munich.

For fourteen years he steered his party through all the obstacles along the way, worked tenaciously and untiringly to overcome all the perils he encountered, until, despite all the set-backs, one success after another began to attach itself to its flying banners. Not because right was on its side; right can be peverted. Not because his followers fought for the final victory with a blind belief and a holy fanaticism — even the greatest sacrifices of life and property can be made in vain. Not because his opponents, driven by hatred and blind fury, committed unforgivable errors in their destructive bent. The Movement triumphed because Adolf Hitler stood at its head, because he is the Movement, because he embodies in his being the idea of National Socialism.

Today Germany is free. The Germany which suffered from shame and disgrace, which Jews and deserters had made the laughing stock of the world, has sunk into oblivion. Like a spectre the years of external enslavement, internal strife, persecution and suppression of Germanness in our country itself, and corruption of an unprecedented scale in all domains of public life have flown away. What our country has dreamt of for centuries has become a reality. A united German Reich has arisen. Class hatred and snobbery have disappeared. United in brotherly love and striving towards one goal, the German nation obeys one command.

All this is the work of Adolf Hitler. And had he achieved nothing more than the following: to win back for the German nation, which for a decade and a half had lain defenceless on the ground, its chisel for ever his name in the Parthenon of History.

If one bears in mind the courage and belief, the endless willingness to make sacrifice, and the devotion which remained alive in all the long years of the struggle to power, beginning with a small group of faithful followers which grew and grew until it became a national movement and finally an army of millions in its brown uniform of honour; if one asks oneself: why have thousands blindly and cheerfully obeyed his every word for ten years or more, putting aside their jobs and their families, suffering scorn and derision, putting up with insults, giving up their last hard-earned pennies silently and without expecting a word of thanks? Why have tens of thousands bowed under the blows of brutish opponents and hundreds encountered death with a last "Heil Hitler" on their pale lips? Why have mothers, whose last and dearest were taken from them, said: "I am proud of this sacrifice"? When one asks oneself how it was possible that a single strong and united movement was formed from this jungle of parties and interest groups, a movement which was above class differences and artificially created rivaleries between people from different parts of the country, above all religious conflict and the most diverse conceptions of what a state should be — then again and again there is only the one answer: because Adolf Hitler was the Fuhrer of this Movement. The brilliant organiser, the fascinating orator and master of propaganda, whom many an arrogant intellectual liked to write off as the "drummer", but who in reality had always been the born statesman. The daredevil with the glowing spirit who looked danger boldly in the face and marched up towards it. The man who calmly weighed the possibilities and knew to wait until the time was right. The man of superior ability who saw through the tricks of his opponents and scattered them far and wide. The generous and kind-hearted man who is compassionate and understanding towards eveyone and was always ready to help if it was in his power to do so. He gave the Movement he created its philosophical basis, the quintessence of his political and philosophical knowledge, born in the hard years of apprenticeship and hardship which characterized his youth, and refined and hardened in the heavy barrage of the World War.

This unique solidarity of the Movement with its Fuhrer cannot be described more vividly than in the words of Rudolf Hess who, at the opening of the congress of the Reichsparteitag in 1933 in Munich, the Congress of Victory, said: "My Fuhrer! As leader of the Party you were to us guarantor of victory. When others wavered, you remained steadfast. When others pointed to a compromise, you remained unyielding. When others' courage failed, you spread new courage. When others left our midst,you seized the flag more determinedly then ever."

Adolf Hitler has never stopped to consider himself. The way he marched at the head of the procession from the Burgerbraukeller which broke up in the teeming rain at the Feldherrnhalle, and the way in which he apprehended the traitors on that unfortunate morning in Wiessee acco—mpanied by only a few loyal supporters, are two examples which show that the entire history of the Party is a single example of the Fuhrer's tremendous personal intervention and boundless devotion to his work. For him there was no rest, no holiday. A fourteen hour or even sixteen hour day were not rare for him. Whole nights were spent in dictation and designing appeals, leaflets and posters. Then he was back again in his car, the train or a plane. Adolf Hitler's own oratorical achievement as he addressed up to four mass gatherings on the one day in different cities cannot be surpassed in human terms. There is no village or town to which he is not tied by some memory. Such memories include threatening crowds of misled countrymen who persued his car with muffled murmurings or with wild shouting or who threw stones --- Masses of people packed together who showed him their love and admiration with tumultuous shouts of "Heil Hitler" and showered him with flowers --- Overflowing village inns in which a few hundred people broke out in thunderous applause, and bursting town halls in which tens of thousands responded in the same way to his speeches --- Blond children lifted into his car by trusting mothers --- Or the modest lantern at an airport which glowed for him like a guiding star after an eerie odyssey in the thick fog.

The Memorial to the Memory of the Men who died at the Feldherrnhalle in Munich on the 9th November, 1923.

Reich's Party Day 1934. The Unveiling of the Standards.

Once a decision was pending and votes had been cast, then the Fuhrer spent the whole night in front of the radio and waited for the results with his followers. Their hearts pounding and holding their breath, they sat and waited for the individual reports to come in. These were written down, calculations were made, conclusions were drawn, and, when then the carefully estimated figures had been reached and when even the boldest expectations had then been sur—passed, the cries of joy that could be heard knew no bounds.

However, there were also days of failure and setbacks. And yet the Fuhrer never lost heart. Not once did he let his courage flag. When he himself, after unprecedented successes, came out with the slogan: "The battle will continue at once!", he stated the same words all the more emphatically when the goal at hand was not reached. When in the November elections in 1932 the National Socialist votes showed a decline compared to the previous election, Adolf Hitler threw himself straight away — and it was way past midnight — with energy and determination into the preparations for the next onslaught. He thought of ways and means of greatly increasing the already quite powerful propaganda machine of the Party in order to reserve this trend the next time.

The Re-enactment of the historical March on
the 9th November 1934.

The head of the old combatants on the 9th November
1935 in front of the Brown House in Munich.

At times the physical and mental vigour of Adolf Hitler seemed to go beyond the bounds of possibility. After a strenuous night trip from Berchtesgaden once he arrived very early in the morning at his hotel in Bayreuth, when there was a telephone call to inform him of the news of the crisis which had been unleashed by the revolt of the SA leader Stennes, and which had already assumed threatening proportions. There was not stopping him. He jumped straight back into his car and raced to Berlin. Here there were discussions and negotiations until the evening, followed by addresses to all the branches of the SA. That same night he set off to return to Munich. He went straight to the Brown House. From here the rebellion had to be put down once and for all. Impromptu dictations into the machine, special editions, leaflets, meetings, all this until late into the night again.

And once more an attempt to split the Movement had been quashed.

This is Adolf Hitler.

This relentless work for the well-being of the Movement and the continual concern for its fate have accompanied Adolf Hitler through all the long years of the struggle. From this work, this incessant struggle, need and deprivation and the torturous worries that are always present, he himself has grown to the massive stature in which today he stands before Germany and the world.

Reichsparteitag 1934.

On the 9th November 1934 in front of the Feldherrnhalle. The Fuhrer with his Deputy, Rudolf Hess, and former combatants.

Reichsparteitag 1935: At the Labour Service on the Zeppelinwiese.

Whoever has been with him in times of the severest difficulties, on days in which the exist—ence and non-existence of the Movement hung in the balance, knows that this man is at his greatest when the moment requires of him a split second decision; he also knows that for this man there is no safe retreat, but that, as has been the case up to now and will always be so in the future, the hour of danger will always find him at the focal point of events and at the head of his following.

Whoever has seen the man at such moments also knows that this man, who radiates bound—less goodness, becomes hard and pitiless if his work is disturbed or his Movement threatened with danger.

Adolf Hitler is generous as no other man has been. He, who has re-established the right of the individual in Germany, wants no lackeys. He wants upright men around him who are used to thinking for themselves, who are willing to take on responsibility and act at their own discretion. He appreciates frank words, and his superior insight is always open to the compelling logic of convincing reasoning. Because he has no use for minions, and wants to encourage the develop—ment of individuals, he gives his co-workers the greatest freedom of action imaginable. He finds petty restrictions and constrictions in other people's work distasteful. He sets the main guide—lines, and shows the direction, but he leaves the individual the greatest room to move. He applies

143

A former combatant: The Fuhrer extends his best wishes
on the occasion of the birthday of General
Litzmann (dec.) in 1934.

standards as far as character and achievement are concerned, not to details of how? and where? and when? and not to tiresome formulae which he has come to detest. He is therefore also ready at any time to forgive mistakes. He turns a blind eye if people occasionally are wide of the mark or err in their choice of tactics. Often with the greatest patience and forebearance he overlooks personal faults and shortcomings to which all human beings are prone.

But woe betide anyone who shakes the fundamental principles of the Movement! Woe betide anyone who dares to abuse the spirit of the Movement and to destroy the essential struct— ure of its organization. Woe betide anyone who has pledged his loyalty to the Fuhrer and the Movement and who breaks this loyalty! For him there is no pardon. There are no exceptions here. Neither rank nor name are taken into consideration. The services, however great, he may have rendered do not weigh heavily enough; his scales fall and he sinks back into the nothingness from whence he came.

Like the wanderer who has made his arduous way to the steep summit of the mountain and looks back on his path which winds its way up through hills and dales, so Adolf Hitler can look back today from his lofty standpoint as the Fuhrer of Germany onto the path which in a fourteen year struggle has led him to the head of the nation. The ascent has been unprecedented, abundant in danger, sacrifices, trials and tribulations, but also abundant in faith, in happiness and in proud inner satisfaction.

And Adolf Hitler likes to look back often, because he has in rich measure something which has always characterized the truly great: gratitude. Gratitude to the Providence whose workings may at times have seemed puzzling and incomprehensible, but which nevertheless fatefully showed the only correct path; gratitude also to his Movement and to his former fellow com—batants, who remained faithful to him in good and bad times. He knows them all personally, he shakes their hand sincerely and joyfully whenever he happens to meet them somewhere in the country, and they can always be sure of his solicitude and his sympathy. A particularly warm friendship binds him to his old SA and SS men. The soldier in him has always found the right words for the combat group in the Party who have been raised in the spirit of soldiers. The combat movement which the National Socialist Party once was in the beginning attracted these combat natures like a magnet. In the early days of the Movement, when the SA was slowly developing from the ranks of the party, which itself had first been formed by a handful of the Fuhrer's comrades-in-arms, Adolf Hitler was seen in the midst of them. He demonstrated with them in the streets, he went with them to the gatherings of the opposition where his comments never missed the mark. When they were out of town he shared with them the straw mattresses in the camps, and when the red mob howled down the demonstration procession in Koburg, he was in the thick of the fray and himself dealt out powerful blows.

Party Day of Freedom. The Fuhrer awaits the Brown Convoys.

The Blood Flag of 1923 at the Reichsparteitag in Nuremberg.

But just as Adolf Hitler continually gives the Party renewed stimulation and strength, his spirit and his blood flow and pulsate through the huge organism which is the Party, so, on the other hand, his Movement is a constant source of strength to him. It is his home. It is the ground in which his whole being has taken root. Just as the National Socialist Movement is unthinkable without Adolf Hitler, so the Fuhrer himself is unimagineable without this Movement. Quite apart from the fact that it was only with this Movement and through this Movement that he created the basis which enabled him to seize the helm of Germany's destiny and step by step to transform his ideas and plans into reality: the Movement and his concern with it have become so much a part of his being that he could not live without it. Even if the burden of office today takes up the greatest part of Adolf Hitler's time and leaves him with less time to concern him—self with the issues of the Party, he still manages to take an active part in all the events which involve the whole organisation and is constantly in touch with the men who hold leading pos—itions in the Party.

The 9th November 1935 in Munich. The Fuhrer speaks with a
party member, the wife on one of the men killed in action on
the 9th November 1923. In the background the Brown House.

A historic place. The Fuhrer and Dr. Goebbels visit the room
in the Sterneckerbrau which served as the first official
quarters of the Party in 1920.

It is no wonder that today also, as Chancellor of the German people, he should feel at home in their midst. Many a time he has acted as a witness at the marriage ceremony of one of his soldiers, many a times he has honoured a member of the Party by consenting to become a godparent to his son. Many a time he has invited SA comrades to his house for a meal or enter—tained them in the Reich's Chancellery! Many a time he has also sought them out when they gathered together on the occasion of anniversary celebrations in their traditional restaurants or even in the dining room of the Brown House. When on these occasions old and young sat around him in their brown shirts, their faces beaming, then Adolf Hiter was, as he had been before, one of them, a friend among friends.

It is these human traits in particular which have engraved the picture of the Fuhrer into the hearts of millions. A nation can be compelled to obedience. A nation will gladly and freely give to a man in his position the respect earned by an exceptional achievement. However, no power on earth can command the love and admiration the Fuhrer enjoys. Nor does this arise spontan—eously. It has its roots only in the personality of Adolf Hitler. It is his personality which sweeps people up and keeps them captive once they have been touched by his spirit; His personality is the fountain from which the hesitant draw courage, the weak draw strength and the doubting draw new hope.

Preparations for the Reich's Party Day of 1935. The Fuhrer discusses the planned march.

Whenever he is tired and weary the contact with the Movement revives him. Whenever he takes the podium at a National Socialist gathering and begins to speak, when he sees the thous—ands of trusting eyes turned to him in expectation, then the spark, which he ignited and which touched the crowds, returns to him and gives him renewed vigour, filling him again with a new will to act. This continual living stream which flows back and forth between the Fuhrer and his followers, which emanates from him and radiates back to him, is perhaps the final secret in the success of Adolf Hitler and therefore in the success of the National Socialist Movement.

This fateful linking of Adolf Hitler and the Movement, this mutual bond which welds one to the other, is the reason why even today Adolf Hitler is drawn as if by magical powers to the historical places associated with the Movement and to all the familiar spots to which he is etern—ally bound by indelible memories. And sometimes a feeling of quiet melancholy may come upon him when he thinks of the times now past when it was still difficult to be a National Socialist.

In an old house in the Sterneckerga chen in Munich, in an unprepossessing little corner, there is the small dark room which had served as the party headquarters in the early days of the Movement and which, after the seizure of power, and at the wish of the Fuhrer, was restored to its former state for the sake of posterity. When Adolf Hitler, at a time when he was already Reichschancellor, after a meeting with his old guard in the neighbouring guard room again entered this room, which could hardly be called room, he found as before on the walls the large red posters on which he had called upon the population of Munich with rousing manifestos to attend the gatherings of the NSDAP. These were the large red posters with the words which struck the first blow at the prevailing popular opinion which had been poisoned by Marxism and which gradually attracted greater and greater crowds in front of the advertising columns in

A visit to the Festung Landsberg in 1934.

Adolf Hitler visits his Leibstandarde (personal body guard).
Next to the Fuhrer is SS Group Leader Josef Dietrich.

Munich, until finally they were banned by the police on the grounds that they were obstructing the traffic. Here he found again all the early leaflets he had written himself and in which he had attacked mercilessly all the adversaries of the German people. And old pictures came to life again and passed before his mind's eye. It was in this poorly lit room that he had sat and fought his initial tough battle to assert himself against the committee of the young party. This had consisted of men who, with the best intentions, were difficult to convince of the fact that if the Movement were to tackle the problem of Marxism it needed the ear of the public, or in other words, the ear of the workers, the 'proletariat', and that, in order to achieve this aim, it had to rely on propaganda. Finally reason triumphed because the popularity of Adolf Hitler continued to grow and the success of the views he represented could not be denied. Thus the young party was spared the fate of sinking into oblivion as an insignificant organization. It became a Movement which filled more and more people with an idea, until it showed a different face to Germany because now it had a Fuhrer.

Reich's Party Day 1935. Consecration of the standards
and honouring the dead.

The 9th of November, 1935, on the Konigsplatz in Munich.
The Leibstandarte (personal body guard) of the Fuhrer.

The 9th November, 1933, marked the tenth anniversary of the day Adolf Hitler made his desperate attempt to change the fate of Germany. Dishonoured and defenceless our fatherland faced a world of enemies. Seized with internal strife, powerless and without unified will, it was at the mercy of a swarm of lascivious preying mutineers. The insanity of inflation, in which there was nevertheless method, was hurling the country ceaselessly towards a catastrophe. Like hyenas and yet wearing the mask of honest men, the separatists crept around the country wait—ing only for the moment in which they could realize their sinister goals and destroy the German Reich once and for all. If something were not done now then it would be too late. And Adolf Hitler acted. The attempt was unsuccessful, the uprising failed. It failed not only because traitors put the stigma of shame upon its name; Now, ten years later, the Fuhrer recognizes the workings of a kindly Providence in this blow of fate. Would the Movement, which at that time was still in its infacy, have been able to fulfil its historical task if the coup had succeeded? At that time the idea of National Socialism had not yet filled the German people to such an extent that a thor—ough revolution in their thoughts and a complete dissolution of the old system could have ensued from a radical political change. Idealism alone cannot build a government. The time was not yet ripe. The Movement did not yet fill all the requirements for the takeover of power in the gover—nment. Yet despite this the march in Munich on the 9th of November had to take place. Despite this the first martyrs of the Movement had to sacrifice their young lives at the Feldherrnhalle. Their blood sowed the seeds of the future all over Germany.

It was an impressive celebration which held the whole of Munich in its spell on this fateful day for the Movement and for the German nation. The evening before had seen the old combat—ants united in the historic room of the Burgerbraukeller from where the uprising had begun. Here the Fuhrer had called for the national revolution, having penetrated the function of the League of Patriotic Organizations during the speech of von Kahr, the Bavarian state commis—sioner. Here there could still be seen the trace of the pistol shot which he had fired as a signal to take cover. Here Kahr, Lossow and Seisser had confirmed their co-operation in the new national government by searing an oath which they broke a few hours later in such a despicable way. The Fuhrer thought of that great moment, and then he thought back over the years which followed and which, through battle after battle, had finally led to victory. For a long time Hitler remained sitting with his friends and exchanged words, greetings and glances with each one.

The Fuhrer on the Party Day of Freedom. Inspection of
the Guard of Honour of his Leibstandarte.

The next morning he again gathered his former combatants around him. They lined up as they had done ten years ago. All wore only the simple brown shirt. Then the historical parade took up its position at the Ludwigsbrucke and marched through the decorated streets of the city to the Feldherrnhalle. At the Odeonsplatz, surrounded by great crowds of people, stood the brown and black convoys in what seemed interminable rows. In front of them the standards had taken up their position. It was an unforgettable moment when the procession arrived and the Fuhrer himself, filled with emotion, then spoke very moving words in honour of the first martyrs of the German revolution. Thereupon he descended the steps of the Feldherrnhalle with measured tread and walked up to the newly erected memorial from which the cover fell. This shattering atmosphere continued as the large wreath slide from his hand to the marble plaque with the splendid greeting: "Victory was yours nevertheless!" Day and night since this solemn occasion the two honour guards of the SS in their steel helmets have been standing watch at either side of the memorial, and everyone who walks past reverently raises his arm in the German greeting. The following year this day was also observed with solemnity, and so it shall be for ever more, as is the wish of the Fuhrer.

About a visit to the Festung Landsberg — 10 years after the Fuhrer and his followers had been held prisoners there for over a year — SS Brigadefuhrer Julius Schaub, one of his oldest fellow combatants and constant companions, writes as follows:

"After the truly heroic struggle which led to the historic breakthrough of the national revolution, the Fuhrer wanted to pay a visit to the Landsberg am Lech prison in which he spent over a year and where the greatest part of his book 'Mein Kampf' was written.

The afternoon of the 7th of October 1934, one of those sunny, clear days which occur only in autumn, saw the Fuhrer, Maurice the present town councillor and SS Oberfuhrer and myself sitting in a car bound for Landsberg. Maurice and I had both been with the Fuhrer in the fortress of Landsberg.

The leaves swirled before us in the autumn wind as we made our way via Pasing, past the Ammersee to Bavarian Swabia. The car which accompanied us was sent on ahead to announce the Fuhrer's impromptu visit so that we could drive into the fortress without creating a sensation.

During the journey memories of those earlier days in Landsberg were renewed. The closer we got to the town the clearer all the experiences which ten years earlier had characterized the lives of the prisoners in Landsberg came into focus. Names like Hess, Kriebel, Weber, Kallenbach, Fischer, Froschl etc. came up. We spoke of Mufti, for so we had christened the prison adminis— trator to whom our well-being in Landsberg was entrusted. And when in the distance the gates and walls of the magnificent old town emerged the Fuhrer told us about his release a few days before Christmas in 1924, how he was picked up by Adolf Muller in an old Benz and photo— graphed standing next to the car infront of the gate we were now approaching.

We then drove through the gate into the town and slowly down a steep narrow street to the splendid market place. Our visit was so surprising that only a few people in the street recognized the Fuhrer. The drive continued through the town and out over the Lechbrucke. Then to the right of us in the countryside there emerged the rooves of the prison lying in the countryside like a little fortress built in the usual star form. A narrow street which passes rows of little houses leads to the entrance of the prison. The wives and children of the prison officials, having been rapidly informed of the news of the Fuhrer's coming, had assembled with bunches of flowers they had quickly plucked from their gardens.

Now the Fuhrer alighted and went under the great portal through which he had first entered the fortress on the 11th of November 1923.

The prison officials, of whom there are still a few who were in office there at that time, were visibly shaken upon seeing the Fuhrer again. Great bunches of keys clanged. It was the same familiar sound we had heard in the bleakness and monotony of our imprisonment when the days crept past in our narrow cells and we were told to turn out our lights, the doors were locked and the steps of the warder gradually faded into the distance as he moved along the corridor. Slowly, with Maurice and myself at his side, the Fuhrer walked along the path which ten years ago he had trodden many hundreds of times, the path on which many thoughts had come to him which today have taken shape and become reality. The path lead around the church of the fortress and past a wing of the prison which was also filled with men from Hitler's raiding party when the prison was overcrowded.

The Fuhrer surrounded by his closest co-workers on the
evening of the Reichstag elections of the 29th March, 1936.

153

Behind this wing and connected to it by a low two-storey building lies the house of the prison institution. When we turned the corner the Fuhrer stopped instinctively for a minute. One of the windows up there belonged to cell no. 7 which had been his abode for a year.

An official who went on ahead unlocked the narrow door which leads into the corridor of the prison. Flowers had been placed on the tables and garlands wound around the doors. This wing of the prison is no longer in use. It is kept as an historic memorial, an outward sign that the spirit cannot be killed by chains and that it is during imprisonment that men, who are supposed to be destroyed there, find the strength to take up the struggle anew and carry it on until the victorious end. A narrow staircase leads up to the first floor where the Fuhrer, Rudolf Hess, Lieutenant Colonel Kriebel and the leader of the Oberland alliance had been housed.

The doors of the individual cells open out onto a corridor. Above cell no. 7 a plaque has been placed in memory of the Fuhrer's term of imprisonment. On the table is a visitor's book in which the Fuhrer now entered his name with a steady hand almost ten years after having left Landsberg. For a long time the Fuhrer stood in his former cell. As he stood at the window through which so often he had looked over the walls into the Swabian countryside, Heinrich Hoffmann captured this historic visit on film. He then showed us a photo which had been taken ten years ago in the same spot.

The Fuhrer now went out to the other part of the prison where the visitor's room was situated. Here he was often visited by former combatants who kept the organisation going outside and created in the Great German National Community a small but powerful strike troup on which later he could at once rely again.

The National Socialist Formations stationed on the almost completed Konigsplatz on the 9th November, 1935.

Photo taken during his term of imprisonment in the Festung Landsberg.

The Fuhrer's visit ten years later. At the window of his cell.

At a conference during the years of struggle. A speaker is
speaking as the Fuhrer makes brief notes. (From l to r)
First Row: Hess, Rust, the Fuhrer, Zorner, Kerrl.
Second Row: behind Hess Schreck (dec.)

The sun was already close to setting as the Fuhrer stepped out again into the courtyard. Everything was as it had been before. Nothing had been changed out of reverence for the Fuhrer. Along the wall there ran a small path which had been christened the Adolf Hitler-Walk. When the other prisoners passed the time with noisy games, the Fuhrer would walk up and down here, lost in thought or deep in conversation with a friend.

Dusk was slowly falling as we returned to the gate. It was a warm farewell which the Fuhrer bad the old officials who still had not been able to compose themselves and who were almost speechless at the thought that the man they once looked after now stood before them as the Fuhrer of the Reich.

In Landsberg in the meantime the rumour had spread that the Fuhrer was there. When we drove back into the town it was overcrowded with people who did not want to miss this opport— unity of seeing the Fuhrer for themselves. Only very slowly could the car make its way ahead through the cheering people. They stood shoulder to shoulder and filled the market place and the steep narrow road which led up to the gate. What a reunion it was! Ten years ago we pris— oners in the fortress secretly produced a small satirical paper with the title 'The Free Citizen of Landsberg'. Today, ten years later, this title is a reality: the former enforced citizen Adolf Hitler has become a free citizen of the town of Landsberg and the whole population of the town is cheering him on.

Higher up near the gate at the spot where one cold, grey winter day next to Adolf Muller's car was taken the historic photo showing the Fuhrer at the start of a new period of his life, we stopped again. And this moment also was captured on film by Heinrich Hoffman.

In the meantime it was growing darker and darker and we drove into the evening back to Munich. Now a silence had descended upon us in the car. Each one of us, filled with the great events of the last ten years and aware of the miraculous change which had taken place, was deep in his own thoughts. Much that had been born in the quiet solitude was now a reality. And be— yond the walls of the fortress the German people had been given their most magnificent present by the Fuhrer: peace."

The Fuhrer has always displayed a very special interest in the Party Days of the NSDAP. They were always the conspicuous expression of the greatness and unity of the Movement. They gave us the great military parades to which all the brown shirted combatants from all the gaus in Germany streamed. They were and are the milestones by which the development and growth of the Movement can be measured. If the first Party Day in Munich in January 1923 was still a more or less local affair, then the next one which took place three and a half years later in Wei— mar showed Germany and the world that the so-called defunct Movement was alive and, sum— moning all its strength, struggling for its resurrection. The fact that, after the Party Days of 1927 and 1929 had been held in historic Nuremberg, Adolf Hitler should declare that from now on the old Durer town would be the city of the Reich's Party Days is typical of the Fuhrer's wish that the Movement should create its own tradition.

The SA motor cyclists drive past the Fuhrer on the Reich's Party Day in 1935.

The preparation for every single Party Day down to the smallest detail has always been a task to which the Fuhrer has devoted himself. During his years of struggle he repeatedly put himself heavily into debt to find the means necessary to enable as many SA as possible to take part. He has always specified the contents of the programme himself. He has always drawn up the guidelines for the various special sessions in which the most diverse issues, such as those concerning youth, women, students, and local politics, were treated in seminar and discussion groups. He has always personally supervised the extensive preparations which transport, housing and the welfare of the masses necessitated. The organisation of the special trains, the preparation of the camps, the allocation of the supply contracts for the mass catering and later the setting up of field kitchens were all questions whose importance grew as the size of the Reich's Party Day reached enormous proportions. Countless times the Fuhrer and his staff have gone to Nuremberg to satisfy themselves on the spot as to the state of the preparations. Until finally the curtain went up and the eager crowds were offered the powerful spectacle which always unfolded in the same setting, but which presented new impressions of incredible beauty and force each time. The Fuhrer considered it his bounden duty to keep one row amidst the great number of honoured guests for the very oldest party members, as well as for the families of men who had died for the cause, so that they would have the opportunity of taking part in these festive days.

Of course it was only after the victorious revolution that the Fuhrer was able to take the measures required to shape the Reich's Party Day entirely according to his will. Initially work was begun to remodel the great square in Luitpodhain which is destined for the roll call of the SA and the SS and the consecration of the flags. Then, on the Zeppelin Field, where since 1933 the march past of the political leaders has taken place, an enormous tribune was erected overshadowed by a gigantic eagle.

The Fuhrer's powerful project for the future, however, which arose from his initiative, and which in the meantime has now been started and will be completed in eight years, will be a cultural memorial to the National Socialist Movement. In its gigantic proportions it will bear witness to coming generations of the victorious omnipotence of the Idea which is embodied in these proud buildings.

**The Fuhrer with the Workers on the Zeppelin Field in
Nuremberg. Reich's Party Day 1935.**

A new city is growing on the party's site in the south west of Nuremberg. With its own water and electricity works and its own sewerage system, this city will be completely independ—ent of the city of Nuremberg. On the gigantic campsite tent cities will arise which will be cap—able of accommodating up to 500,000 people. The congress hall whose foundation stone will be laid shortly will seat 65,000 people. For the parading of the Wehrmacht a special field is being prepared which will offer room for 400,000 spectators. Wide, spacious streets and its own rail—way station will cater for the smooth arrival and departure of the masses. Finally an 80—90 metre road will be created for the march past. Its own association containing representatives of the Party and the government, the German Reichsbahn and the city of Nuremberg was estab—lished to ensure these enormous works would be carried out in a uniform way.

It is with joyous pride and inner participation that the Fuhrer follows the progress of his work. Once it has been completed the Reichs Party Day will be, in even greater measure, the point of concentration of the total display of strength of National Socialist Germany and with it the true Reich's Day of the German Nation.

Ten years ago the Fuhrer once remarked: "I will soon have to go to Berlin now, because Berlin is the centre of political life. But the seat of the Movement will always remain in Munich." And he has kept his word. Next to the Brown House, which for years has been a world-wide symbol of National Socialism, and in the vicinity of the numerous other buildings in which the departments of the Reich's leadership are housed, two gigantic buildings, the Fuhrer building and the Administration Building, are emerging as the concrete expression of the will of the Fuhrer. He himself, who still has his residence in Munich and returns to this city which has become his second birthplace, whenever possible, never misses an opportunity to visit the Brown House, the home of his work. Here the conference of the leaders of the Reich take place and here the important discussions of the Party are usually held.

And finally, in order to immortalize the fusion of the party with this city, the Fuhrer has bestowed on Munich the official title "City of the Movement". With this gift he has thanked Munich for the first successes which it granted to his political work, for the sacrifices it brought to the Movement and for the faith it kept in him.

Here is the birthplace of the Movement.

Here it first had to justify its existence.

Here the first brawls took place, the first violent disputes with the Marxist parties.

The ground in front of the Feldherrnhalle is sanctified with the blood of the first martyrs of the National Socialist Idea.

The Fuhrer, 1921.

Here the great trial was held which first carried the name of Adolf Hitler beyond Germany.

Here the NSDAP was founded a second time at a historical place.

From here it began its triumphal march through the whole of Germany.

Adolf Hitler has never been a party leader in the popular sense, just as the NSDAP has never been a party in the sense of other parties. It has only ever been the organisatory core of the great National Socialist Movement which today is the sole political organ representing the will of the German nation. From the beginning its task has been to absorb the many other parties and thus remove the party system altogether in Germany, and to put in its place the National Community. The NSDAP was never an end in itself for Adolf Hitler. From the start he saw in it only the active core division of the German people and beyond it the ultimate goal for which he longed and to which his struggle, his work and his concerns were devoted:—

"GERMANY, NOTHING BUT GERMANY!"

The Fuhrer unfurls the standards on the
Party Day of Freedom.

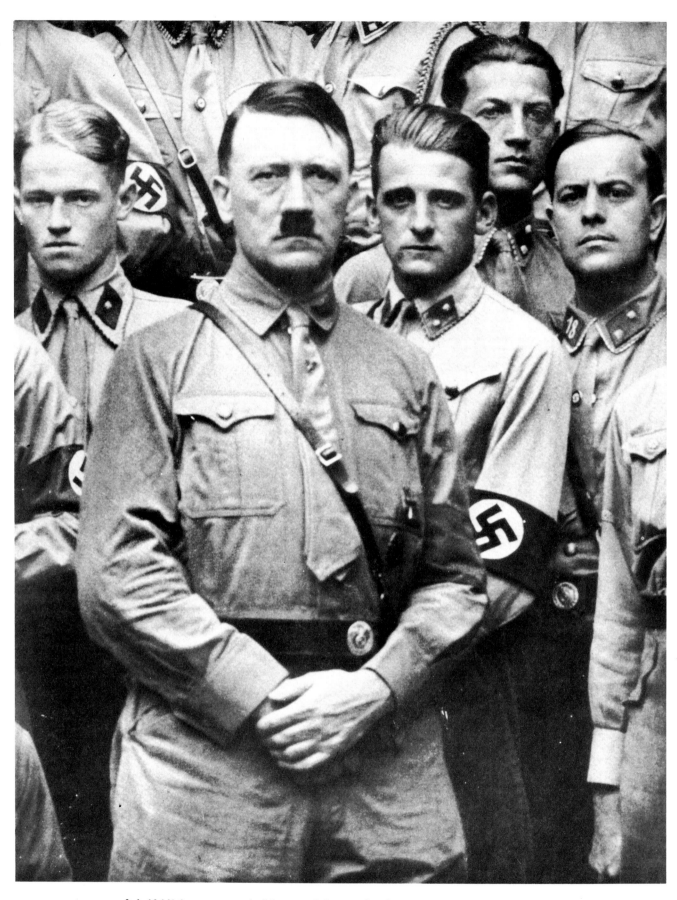

Adolf Hitler surrounded by participants in the leadership school.

"The Almighty gave him the power
To free millions of Germans —
And yet his greatest ambition
Is to be a proper German man."

Girls greet the Fuhrer.

Bavarian children.

The Fuhrer speaks to a wounded
member of the SU.

One of the bravest.

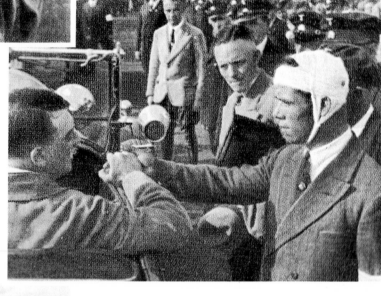

Honour.

Inspecting the troops in Bern.

An historical moment for Cabinet. Hitler greets the marching troops on 30th January, 1933.

Assembly in Dortmund, 1933. Josef Wagner, Wilhelm Schepmann, Adolf Hitler and Lutze, Troop Leaders.

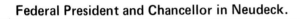

Federal President and Chancellor in Neudeck.

The Fuhrer addresses troops in Dortmund, 1933.

In the midst of campaigning. The Fuhrer discusses his proposed route with flight captain Baur.

There is only one Ideal — that of work (1st May, 1933).

The Fuhrer visits the graves of fallen warriors.

The Fuhrer's house in Upper Salzburg.

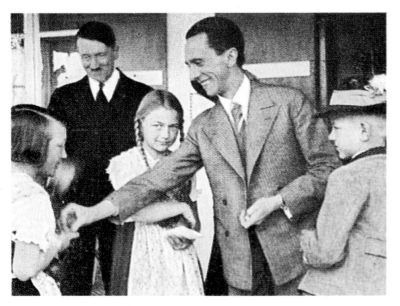

The Fuhrer and Dr. Goebbels in
Upper Salzberg.

The Fuhrer in his study at the Brown House.

German National Day, Nuremberg, 1927

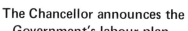

In Potsdam.

The Chancellor announces the
Government's labour plan.

Coburg, 1931.

The Fuhrer and his fans — Nuremberg, 1933.

The Fuhrer is an animal lover.

The Fuhrer.

The Fuhrer speaks.

Trip to Eastern Prussia.

Flight around Germany.

The Fuhrer after a three hour conference.

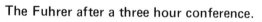

Loved by the people.

The Fuhrer leaves the Brown House.

Chancellor Hitler and Vice - Chancellor von Papen
on the way to mass.

The Fuhrer visits a war ship.

Nuremberg, 1929.

Turning turf at the commencement of work on the
Reichsautobahns (Federal Highways), Frankfurt, 1933.

Germany has awakened! Berliners
cheer the Fuhrer.

The Fuhrer honours a German fighter.

The Fuhrer with the "Blue Boys".

The Chancellor and Admiral Raeder with the German fleet.

The Fuhrer with the Press Director.

Nuremberg, 1923
(Adolph Hitler and Julius Streicher)

Hitler leaves the Marien- Church in
Wilhelmshaven.

The Fuhrer with Professor Troost, architect of
the Brown House.

The Fuhrer in Danzig.

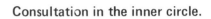
Consultation in the inner circle.

The Chancellor with colleagues, Ministers Goring and Frick.

In Berchtesgaden.